What is it for?

A system approach for value(s) creation

by Olaf de Hemmer Gudme

copyright – 2018 Olaf de Hemmer Gudme
odehemmer@valeursetmanagement.com

Illustration: Caroline Boutrois
caroline.boutrois@gmail.com

To my stakeholders

Olaf de Hemmer Gudme, management consultant and trainer for 30 years has been working for 20 years in value(s) creation in various fields of innovation, purchasing, IT, ... Past President of AFAV, the network of value professionals in France, and founder of the Value(s) & Management network >1300 members), he has implemented this approach in more than 100 projects in all sectors throughout the world.

He published with other 20 experts of corporate performance improvement *"Valeur(s) & Management"*[1] presenting their Value(s) methods. This book aims (utopia?):

- to synthesize the common points of these approaches in a generic meta-method, applicable to all levels and all subjects of the economy
- to show that it works, through concrete examples taken from his experience
- to encourage to implement these elements actors who wish to reconcile economic performance and human happiness: potential synergies are impressive!

---

[1] *Valeur(s) & Management : des méthodes pour plus de valeurs dans le management"* by Olaf de Hemmer and Hugues Poissonnier, EMS Ed° 2013 & 2017

Introduction

How can the economy generate either more value creation and more respect for values?

The key question is "*What is it for?*".

All children discovering the world do ask the same question "*Dad (or Mum), why ...?*". And we –parents- answer it by *"Because ..."* (the explanation). After all, this is the Cartesian thinking underlying science that we have been educated to use! So, we explain the world to our children that way. Haven't you experienced that this answer is often not enough? And the child repeats *"Yes, but why ...?"*. The conversation ending either when the parent does not know more, or the child is tired. But weren't we ignoring what they really were looking for: to understand the world's meaning, its purpose?

The right question would be *"What is it for ...?"* so that the answer would be *"In order to ..."*. Its power is so astonishing that one wonders why we so little use this common sense? This question leads to define meaning, direction, utility, purpose, goals, objectives ... And to common sense: a logical and pragmatic reasoning.

Next time a 6-year-old child asks you *"Why ...?"*, try to answer as if he asked *"What for ...?"*. For example, *"Dad, why is it raining?"*. This would lead to *"Because the cloud is heavy with water."*, *"Yes, but why?"* ... maybe leading the scientist father to: *"Well, the water follows the evapo-transpiration cycle, etc."*. Not sure the child would follow? But if you understood *"Dad, what for is it raining?"*, the answer would be *"To deliver water to flowers so they – and us- can drink"*. Do you see how meaningful it becomes?

And if you still doubt, try to answer: *"What do you think?"*. Probably you'll get something like: *"So that we can jump in the poodles!"*. What a nice occasion to check that purpose is definitely linked to each person's point of view! And to transform a boring science lesson into playful games!

Scientific reasoning allowed us to better understand the word and leads to so much progress!

But let us go beyond Cartesian thinking, based on 'causality', which makes managers short-sighted (short-term vision) and autistic (oblivious to their dependence on their ecosystem), makes them lose meaning (direction) and common sense (intuition), create organizations in silos between which competition prevails, where baronies isolate themselves from the outside...

Let us use System thinking, in which each actor is interdependent with the others, where each one is oriented towards meaning, goals, wishes, which alone move people towards action. Where collaboration and dialogue allow to build processes mobilizing collective intelligence to create the *value* expected by each, while respecting its *values*.

This book will present the application of the 3 principles of Value(s) thinking, and the radical innovations and amazing improvements in value(s) creation it allowed in all areas of business performance: the company and its governance, business units or services, corporate functions, administrative and industrial processes, products, professional training... And it remains relevant outside the company itself: a school educational project, individual time management, and even ... the meaning of life (!).

The collective book "*Valeur(s) & Management*"[2] published in April 2013 and reedited in December 2017 presents some of the Value(s) methods already at work in various areas of business performance: Shared Value, Blue Ocean, BCorps, Eco-design, Value Analysis, Lean, Customer Perceived Value, Corporate Social Responsibility, Business Analysis... or in development: Solution focus coaching, the Interactifs discipline ... Dozens of methods - a real wave! Enough to drown Descartes' "*Discourse of the method*" under a tsunami of value(s)!

---

[2] "*Valeur(s) & Management : des méthodes pour plus de valeurs dans le management*" by Olaf de Hemmer and Hugues Poissonnier, EMS Ed° 2013 & 2017

Value(s) thinking will allow:

➢ Each decision-maker to **do more (good) with less (goods) for more (people)**, at his own responsibility level, in coherence with the corporate strategy / mission / values and with other internal and external actors of the company, by rediscovering common sense and respecting the values of others.

➢ Promoters of the most effective optimization methods in each area to understand how to **work in synergy** with specialists in other areas of business performance, to be even more effective.

This book is built in 4 parts:

- Part 1 – Value(s) thinking
- Part 2 – Common concepts of Value(s) methods
- Part 3 – Applications of Value(s) thinking
- Part 4 – Existing Value(s) methods

Part 1 - Value(s) thinking

The 5-legged sheep

Probably you have already been asked to solve a difficult problem, to meet seemingly contradictory requirements ... In short, to find a real "5-legged sheep"!

Follow me in a small exercise of reflection, which I regularly use to understand the Value(s) thinking principles: if I really asked you to find me a 5-legged sheep, what would be its value?

Please think for a moment before turning the page!

The answers may vary of course according to your definition of "value" ... However, the most common are always the same:

"*A 5-legged sheep is very expensive, since it is rare*", a response full of pragmatic and realistic common sense,

"*A five-legged sheep should be worth a quarter more than a four-legged sheep*" (where a professional purchaser would add than he would negotiate the 5th leg for free),

"*It is not worth anything, since it is a mistake of nature*", generally comes from people who know about sheep farming

Who is right? Is anyone wrong? Difficult to determine a value that is unanimous! It seems that the value of the sheep with 5 legs is very subjective ...

" *It depends!* " is another fairly common answer.

So, what is 'value' depending on? The person who will measure it! How will she determine that a solution will have more value for her? Depending on its perceived usefulness:

> The boss of a circus will be willing to put a lot of money to show a nice little lamb on his 5 legs in his menagerie, since it is rare and he will be the only one!

> The producer of a horror film "*The return of the five-legged sheep*" will be ready to pay dearly but will also be able to rent the sheep to the circus or have a special effects studio add a fifth leg to the picture.

> To give 5 families a leg of lamb, the buyer will not be willing to put more than 25% more than for 4 legs!

> A breeder will want to get rid discreetly and for nothing of a degenerate lamb in his flock, unless he decides to build an amusement park ...

> In Saint Exupéry's story, the "Little Prince" asked the lost aviator to draw him a sheep - with no mention of the number of legs. The aviator, unable to draw anything but open or closed boas, drew a box, in which the Little Prince thought he could find the prettiest sheep to devour the baobabs shoots that threatened his planet, but not its delicate rose! We see here that the answer (a box) to the demand (a sheep) is not necessarily the best way to meet a need (destroy baobab shoots + protect the rose)! And that radical innovations are possible: to do more (good) ofr more (people) with less (resources).

The value of something is:

- relative "it depends! "
- subjective, relative to a person and different according to their point of view

- function of the perceived utility of the user, of the response to his needs, as well as the perceived cost of getting it

This shows the difficulty of giving an objective measure of value for anything! But each user can choose between different solutions the one where he perceives the most value: it is therefore possible to measure the (at least relative) value of different solutions.

The utility of a thing for someone is the answer to the question "**What is it for?** ". This question is the focus of the Value(s) thinking.

This example of the five-legged sheep shows that the value of a thing is also linked to the resources spent: the more the user must consume resources to meet his need, the less the solution has value to him. Between 2 solutions that fulfill his need in an equivalent way, he will choose the one that costs him the least.

The value of a thing is thus not only related to its utility, but also to its cost. We will therefore retain as definition:

$$\textbf{Value(s) = utility(ies) / cost(s)}$$

$$\textbf{Value(s) = satisfied needs / resources consumed}$$

To optimize the value of something requires asking a 2d question: **"What is enough? "**.

What will be enough to fulfill one's need will obviously not suit somebody else: the cheap 5 lamb legs fulfill the need of the 5 families to feed, but not the one of the circus boss!

It should be noted that the most expensive solution is not necessarily the one that best fits the needs of all: buying a live 5-legged sheep, which suits the circus boss need, may be replaced by renting it for the movie shooting, and does not respond correctly to the need to feed 5 families: in addition to paying an expensive sheep, they will have to slaughter it, and will have legs not necessarily similar for each family ...

This trivial example clearly shows the relevance of the two key questions of Value(s) thinking:

- **What is it for?**
- **What is enough**?

A third point is central to Value(s) thinking: with whom do we work? Being based on the 2 questions above, it will be necessary to collaborate with ... the people who know the answers! This reasoning cannot be effectively carried out alone: we'll have to

- **Work with stakeholders**
    - to answer "what is it for? ": users and those who know their true needs

- to answer "what is it enough? ": the actors of the current solution and suppliers of alternative solutions

These 3 simple principles prove surprisingly effective in finding innovative, more efficient and economical solutions. Examples of applications are presented in the following pages.

These concepts, as simple and obvious as they appear, are not spontaneous to most people and are often difficult to implement! The reason is probably that we were educated to think without them!? We are rather trained to systematically implement Cartesian thinking, at the heart of science, basis of the progress of Western civilization. The following pages show that the Value(s) principles are based on another equally strong paradigm: the *'system'* approach.

The 3 Value(s) principles

The Value(s) state of mind assumes to consider everything as a set of resources implemented to meet needs.

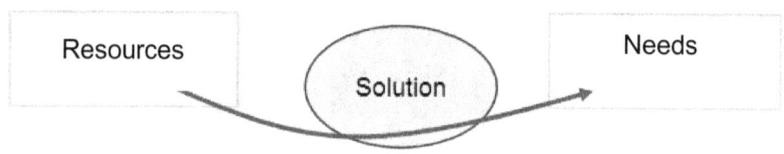

Any problem-solving approach aims at improving the value of an unsatisfactory solution:

- A better satisfaction of stakeholders' needs

- Fewer resources consumed to meet them

To improve the value of a solution, we propose 3 key points: 2 questions and 1 principle

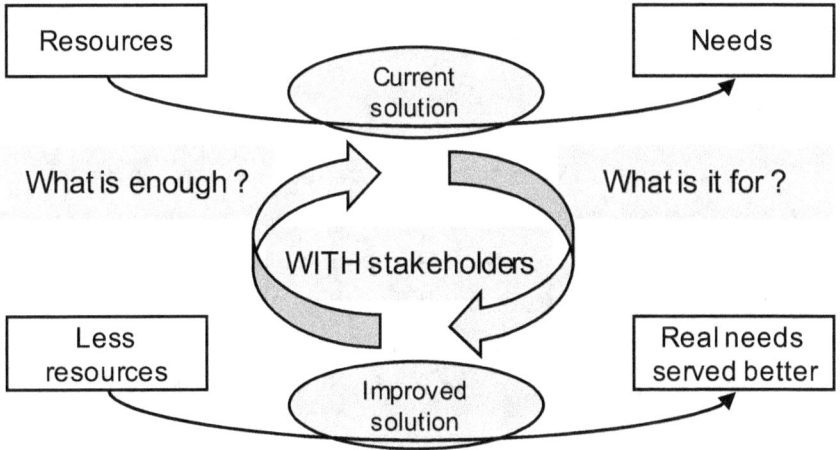

Needs: What is it for?

The reference solution finds its usefulness in its purpose, its 'reason of being': to offer the people who use it the performances they expect, often different according to different users.

At other times of its life cycle, other people expect other performances: prescribers, sellers, buyers, installers, maintainers ... They look for: image, customer impact, ease of storage, ease of maintenance ...

Besides its 'reason of being', the solution implementation also implies resisting constraints and respecting the elements of the natural, artificial and societal environment.

The definition of needs is done with each relevant stakeholder: users, prescribers...

Resources: What is it for?

The solution implements resources that we want to save: usually materials, energy and manpower leading to purchasing costs, but also implementation costs, time consumption, environmental and societal impacts, etc. To know about spent resources, we'll need to work with other stakeholders: designer, suppliers ...

Are these resources implemented to meet the needs? Experience shows that resources often are implemented to answer the needs of other stakeholders than the users: we'll challenge them!

Some of the needs consume a lot of resources: we'll challenge them first.

What is enough?

The search for alternative solutions involves challenging needs and resources with the relevant stakeholders:

Needs :

- ➢ Do all needs contribute to user satisfaction?
- ➢ What happens if we do nothing?
- ➢ Are some needs specific to some users and not all?
- ➢ Are some of the needs already covered by other solutions?

Resources:

- ➢ Does spending contribute to real utility/needs satisfaction?
- ➢ Which solution is sufficient to answer each need?
- ➢ Which solutions exist in other domains to answer the same utility?

The systematic implementation of this questioning is often sufficient to highlight very innovative alternatives.

The direct involvement of stakeholders is paramount: only users can validate their perception of utilities (even if they often have difficulty expressing them!), only suppliers know the cost drivers, and so on. This careful listening to the stakeholders, often excluded from the work because outside the company and project teams, is at the same time a real strong point and the greatest difficulty of this Value(s) thinking approach.

To go further and ensure a systematic approach, especially when participants are not familiar with the approach, tools exist to facilitate the implementation of the concepts. In particular, system modeling makes it easier to answer the questions "*What is it for?*", by highlighting the flows and exchanges between the solution and its environment, leading to the value created and perceived by the stakeholders. It will be presented in the following pages.

The system modeling tool

The system modeling, proposed by Jean-Louis Le Moigne in " *La théorie du système general*"[3] makes it easier to answer the Value(s) thinking questions. These are indeed simple, but their answer is not always easy: we must mobilize different actors, who have to agree to formalize sometimes seemingly contradictory needs, respecting different cultures, languages and values. The construction

---

[3] The elements of system modeling are presented in the following § in application of the principles of the " Théorie du système général " by Jean-Louis Le Moigne. 1977, PUF. Reissued in 1986, 1990, 1994 and 2006 in e-book. (ISBN 2-13038-483-8).
They are found under other names and with some variants of form in many methods like Value Analysis, Value Stream Mapping, business mapping ... We will systematically link to the tools of the analysis value.

of a graphic model, instead of telling opposing points of view, puts everyone in front of the same object and facilitates mutual understanding and collective intelligence. The system approach highlights the relationships between internal and external elements.

1. What is it for?

- *Needs* - **relations between elements:**

Any object of study can be considered as a system that manages relations or flows between two elements, distinct in space with the relation of an actor to a target, or in time by transformation of the characteristics of Inputs into Outputs:

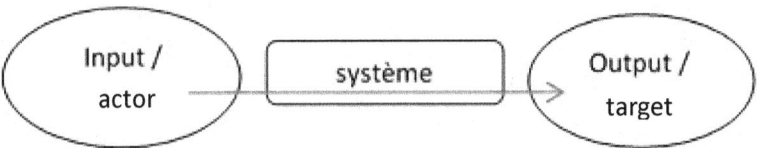

A system generally participates in several relationships between external elements, and is always required to manage interactions with isolated elements:

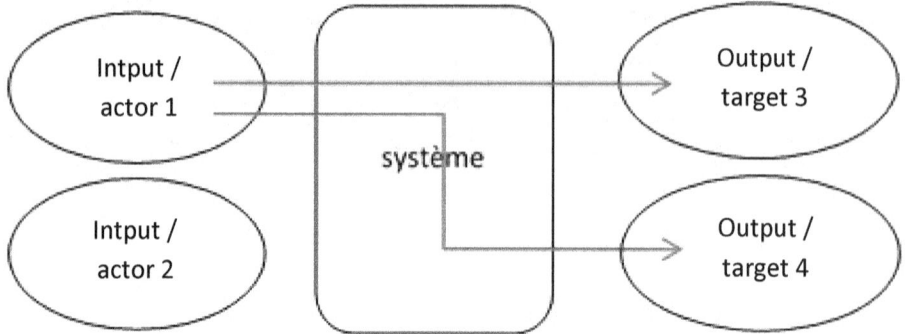

2. Work WITH the stakeholders

- Who is it for?

The value of a system is the perception of the ratio between its utility and the costs it generates. A utility can only be established in relation to at least one person. Thus, modeling is complemented to highlight its relationships with people: each relationship is established either directly between "stakeholders" or indirectly through relationships between physical elements that are themselves related to the stakeholders through Other physical elements:

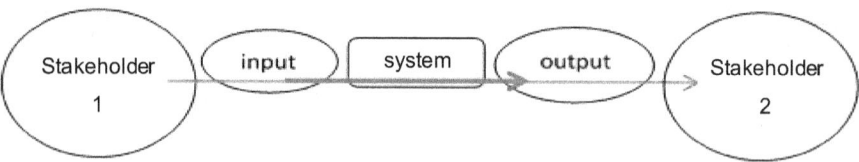

- When? Life Cycle Stages

A system finds its *raison d'être* when it is used, but still manages other flows at different points in its life cycle: it will record its expected performance from its creation to its end of life, The stages of availability, use(s), maintenance, evolutions ... Stakeholders at these stages are different, their expectations are different and the utilities of the system for each of them must be formalized.

Different users can also assign a different utility to a system that manages the same input / output relationship. The system modeling will have to distinguish these different cases.

3. What is enough?

- Actual solution: what is enough today?

One can model in the same way the participation of the components of a system to each flow managed by this one by visualizing which components pass through these flows:

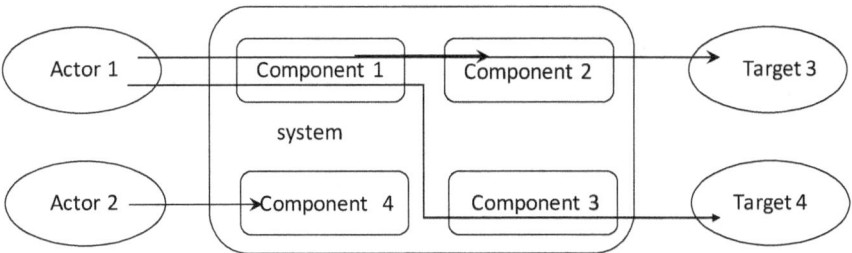

This zoom in system modeling amounts to formalizing the relations managed by each of the components with its own external elements, which may be external to the system considered initially, or other components of this system. In the above modeling, the component 1 manages the 2 flows between the actor 1 and the component 2 and the actor 1 and the component 3.

The costs of a system (in money, time, energy, materials ... direct or indirect ... real or risks...) are linked to the resources necessary to materialize the components. In the modeling above, the cost of the flow management system between actor 1 and target 2 is equal to the costs of components 1 and 2. The costs of the components involved determine the cost of each utility of the system.

- Improved solution: what could be enough?

The value of the system will be optimized by proposing other technical solutions (other components, architectures or sizing within the limits of the system studied) that meet the actual expected performance at the lowest cost.

In the case of a process, the components are the steps of the process, for which resources are implemented:

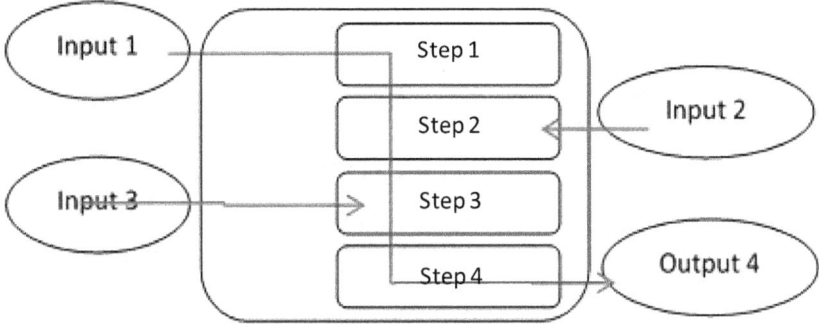

The value of a process is improved by adapting the quality or quantity of outputs produced to the actual needs of the stakeholders, avoiding temporary outputs, limiting the resources consumed ...

System modeling facilitates the expression of needs at different levels: components or steps / solution or situation / system / stakeholders:

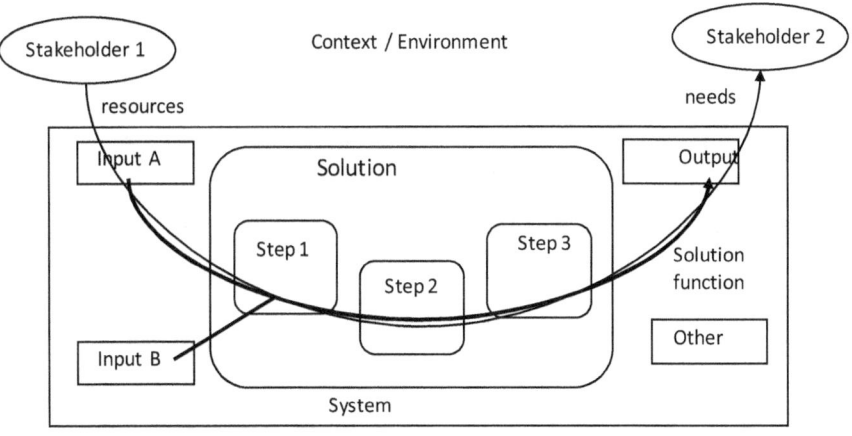

- the function of the solution is to transform the inputs A and B into output,
- by implementing several stages or components,
- to fulfill, along with other elements of the system, the need for a stakeholder (2), from the resources of another stakeholder (1)

Part 2 – Common concepts of Value(s) methods

Let us dream of a company where:

- Strategy would target delivering to each of its stakeholders –investors, customers, employees, suppliers and partners, administration, environment, society and NGOs…- more value = more satisfaction and less costs
- Products and services would enthusiasm actual and future customers, improve employees skills and wellbeing, develop suppliers long term strength
- Each function would be managed with KPIs showing its contribution to these goals and to the success of the other company's functions
- Industrial and information processes would produce only outputs useful to these functions role versus the company's stakeholders, with efficient production and IT systems
- Each actor would bring its time, skills and motivation against not only money but also wellness at work, a sense of personal and collective usefulness, and long term personal achievement
- Each person would achieve its goals by collaborating to others', in the respect of each other's values

A company with more value(s) in management? How is it possible?

These lines conclude the book " *Valeur(s) & Management* »[4], which presents some of the methods implemented in various areas of performance improvement where they contribute to creating more Value(s) in companies: value analysis, blue ocean, eco-design, lean, customer perceived value, corporate social responsibility ...

Each of these methods is based on a specific approach that has often revolutionized its field. Can we highlight it? Could it serve as a meta-method to deploy in all areas of management? Here is the ambition of this book, through the exploration of the common concepts of these methods, their scientific basis and the demonstration that the application of these concepts allows a resolutely original and effective approach.

Value/system methods:

The work carried out with the specialists in the methods presented in the book " *Valeur(s) & Management* " highlighted the principles they share to improve performance:

- The *value* concept, where *value = perceived usefulness / perceived costs,* targets solution improvement by :
    o Improving its usefulness, by answering better to its *purposes/goals* for the different

---

[4] « Valeur(s) & Management : des méthodes pour plus de valeur(s) dans l'entreprise » par O. de Hemmer et H. Poissonnier, Ed° EMS 2013

stakeholders of its *life time* : user, buyer, distributor, manufacturer ...
- Avoiding unuseful spending of resources, not participating to the purposes : money, raw material, time, comfort, security ...
- A *benefits / costs* analysis
- A *system* approach, where each actor is depending from the others :
  - things are defined by their *goal*, modeled from relations with their *environment*
  - in a continuous *flow* of transformation of *inputs* to *outputs*
  - each analysis must be replaced in a global view, integrating the whole *life cycle* and considering different *levels of goals*
  - actors and objects are in continuous *interaction* and evolution
- The importance given to *meaning* and *dialog*
  - every analysis must be made with the people involved or impacted : the *stakeholders*
  - needs have to be expressed by those having them (they often must be helped ...)
  - a change is effective only if it is accepted or – better !- proposed by those who are impacted, and it is implemented with them in short retroactive loops demonstrating results and progressive improvement

A New « Discourse on the Method »

It seems that the commonalities of these methods - developed independently by various specialists - are derived from the new trend of thought carried by the system approach? A new paradigm is developed there that goes beyond Cartesian thinking in the same way that Einstein's relativity has overcome Newton's physics:

Yesterday :

- Newton's physics correctly describes the behavior of objects on our scale,
- Descartes was obviously not wrong in writing the " Discours de la Méthode ", from which emerges the scientific reasoning which has so greatly advanced our society!

Today :

- Einstein has more exactly explained the functioning of matter, of which Newton's physics is only a special case (very useful)!
- The *system* approach[5], in which Western science rediscovers principles already present in Oriental approaches, goes beyond the Cartesian thinking of the

---

[5] *La théorie du système général. Théorie de la modélisation*, Jean-Louis Le Moigne, 1977, PUF. Reedited in 1986, 1990, 1994 et 2006 as a e-book. (ISBN 2-13038-483-8).

Enlightenment, opposing the 4 principles established "to lead well its reason"

The 'cartesian' principles:	The 'system' principles:
> Evidence: knowledge is absolute	> *Relevance: knowledge is relative*
> Analysis: understanding the whole by its parts	> *Globalism: understanding the object by its environment*
> Causality: causes / effects relations	> *Teleology: goals / means relations*
> Completeness: make sure you do not omit any details	> *Agregativity: choose an overall representation*

These system principles are found in the Value(s) methods. The third principle of teleology, especially, refers to the relationship between goals and means: this is the utility, the purpose, the basis notion of value. These principles could be summarized as a way of analyzing, a posture in the analysis of an object:

Descartes considers:	System thinkers consider:
> What's going on inside	> What's going on outside
> Relations between components	> Relations between interactors
> Causes in the past: "why?"	> Goals, towards the future: « what is it for? "

This is another way to look at things:

> Descartes proposes to study the interior of the object of study and the cause-effect relations between its components:

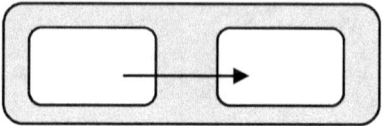

> Le Moigne proposes to study the outside of the object of study and the goals-means relations between the elements of its environment:

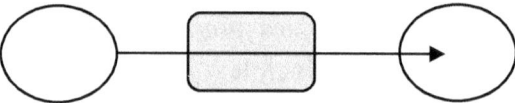

The two approaches are therefore quite complementary. But the system approach allows an open-mindedness and degrees of freedom that we have all too often found to be cruelly lacking in Cartesian thinking!

The systemic approach[6] therefore envisages studying an object under three aspects:

- the *functional* aspect ("what the system does") that is sensitive to the purposes of the system, where one studies

---

• wikipedia 'approche systémique' :
http://fr.wikipedia.org/wiki/Approche_syst%C3%A9mique#La_triangulation_syst.C3.A9mique

the environment without detailing the system itself ("out of the box"

- the *structural* aspect ("how the system is composed") which aims to describe the structure of the system, the arrangement of its various components. This "analytical" approach focuses more on the relationships between components than on the components themselves

- the *historical* (or "genetic" or dynamic aspect: "what the system was or becomes") that is linked to the evolutionary nature of the system, endowed with a memory and a project capable of self-organization, of regulation.

It seems[7], moreover, that the Enlightenment movement responded in the 18th century to the excesses of a clergy refusing the questioning of dogmas (creation in 7 days, heliocentrism ...): the best way to avoid mixing a rigorous reasoning, necessary for the understanding of phenomena, with spiritual considerations, was to remove the question " what is it for? " leading to purpose and transcendence. Besides, Descartes, even if he did not question his faith, wrote a *discourse* on method and not a *treaty*, to avoid the wrath of the Inquisition which had just condemned Galileo

---

[7] « Quand science et foi s'éclairent l'une l'autre », éditorial du n° 43 de *Teilhard Aujourd'hui, par* Gérard Donnadieu, Président de l'Association des amis de Pierre Teilhard de Chardin, http://www.teilhard.fr/files/Revue%20Teilhard/43_Revue_n43.pdf

for the second time. After Rabelais's declaration "Science without conscience is only the ruin of the soul", Descartes separates science and consciousness, as Edgar Morin[8] reminds us: "... *in opposition to traditional science whose effectiveness is based on Separation between the subject and the object, facts and values* ". Since then, scientists and spiritualists have claimed a distinct field of action. Developments in life sciences, cybernetics and computers, as well as in business sciences, have put this question of meaning and purpose back on the agenda. Many scientists argue for a reintroduction of meaning in *semantic* thinking, to complement Cartesian *deterministic* thinking.

What if the system approach made it possible to reconcile the analysis of goals and causes? The two French theorists of systemic thought lay the foundations:

> Jean-Louis Le Moigne in «*La théorie du système général*»[9] establishes the systemic modeling, facilitating the expression of the purposes (functional aspect) and their relation with the components of the solutions (structural aspect)

---

[8] Edgar Morin, « Le Paradigme perdu, la nature humaine » Seuil, Paris, 1973, p.231
[9] Jean-Louis Le Moigne, « La théorie du système général. Théorie de la modélisation », PUF 1977

> Edgar Morin in "*The method*"[10] builds a new paradigm to create "transdisciplinary thinking", emphasizing the considering of complexity, evolution and regulation, interactions between actors (historical and dynamic aspect), emerging properties ...

Value vs Values

Management approaches widely use the terms **'value'** and **'values'** with different meanings and nuances, but these are usually as quite opposed:

> Value = money = wealth, OR = utility
> Values = ethics = caring about people and planet, on the other.

One notes that the company is a mean for stakeholders to exchange what they have against something that will creates **'value'** for themselves:

- Clients exchange money, but also time, comfort, information... In the acquisition process... against a product/service, which will itself create **value** for themselves or their own customers: satisfy physical, intellectual, social status... needs,

---

[10] Edgar Morin, « La Méthode, La Nature de la nature (t. 1) », 1977 Le Seuil, Nouvelle édition, coll. Points, 1981

- Vendors exchange the same product/service, but also marketing and supply chain costs and time... against money, but also reputation, long term relationship...
- Each of them perceives more **'value'** in what he gets than what he gives, even if the same is given and received on both sides! If not, the exchange will not happen (or at least not last long). So the exchanged **'valueS'** are subjective and relative to each stakeholder.

The same applies to exchanges with other stakeholders in the company:

- ➤ Employees: money, relations, work conditions, career ... against time, skills, motivation ...
- ➤ Suppliers: products / services, stable supply in quality / costs / delays, innovations, market information ... against money, payment deadline, strategic visibility ...
- ➤ Shareholders: dividends -expected? -, resale price of the share, image, industrial synergies ... against investment -passed! -, managerial involvement ...
- ➤ But also the environment: which expects at least to be respected in return for the provision of living conditions, air, water ...
- ➤ And society: waiting for employment, local economic impact, taxes ... against the provision of infrastructures, education, security ...

When it comes to exchanges with people (it always is!), the company may not respect them, but taking the **'values'** of customers, suppliers, employees, society ... into account certainly is part of the exchange of '**value**' with them! This show **value** and **values** more like sources of opportunity and synergy more than opposite.

Each company is built on the choice –explicit or implicit- to consider certain stakeholders **value(s)** as a priority: the neo-liberal public-owned company usually focuses on shareholders short term profit by share value, while social entrepreneurs choose employment of specific publics as a priority, profit becoming a 'constraint' for long term growth ... So even if one of their stakeholders get priority, every company HAS to deal with the satisfaction of EACH of its stakeholder to secure its sustainable future!

It therefore appears that *value* and *values* are more sources of opportunity and synergy than in opposition?!

Value(s) methods give central importance to meaning and dialogue with stakeholders or stakeholders: users, suppliers, etc. Exploring needs and solutions around system modeling allows a dialogue between stakeholders to imagine improvements:

- *users* will express their needs and validate the utilities of the future system
- *designers* will validate the participation of the system components in the utilities
- *actors involved* in the solution will validate the changes required for them

- other responses to utilities will be defined, through various forms of creativity
- the best solution for the future system will be chosen: the one corresponding to the user-defined utilities, at the lowest costs defined by the designers.

This dialogue with stakeholders implies the most direct contact possible and true listening, based on mutual respect, in particular respect for possibly different values between people whose interests may seem divergent (buyer, seller, user, manufacturer, Supplier ...) but must be completed simultaneously! The creation of value is done by an exchange respectful of the values of each one.

These general principles can be applied to the optimization of all kinds of study objects: products, industrial or tertiary process, business model, organization, professions, communication ... We will study them in the next § and make the link with the Methods which specifically aim at their optimization. The system modeling makes it possible to find the foundations and sometimes to supplement them.

Giving people a sense of purpose and humanity

The major lesson of this work is that each decision-maker can implement one or more of these Value(s) methods in his / her field, improve, combine them and implement them with powerful synergies:

> ➢ A *Blue Ocean* strategy can be realized
> ➢ with a *Radical Innovation Design* approach,

- Leading to products optimized by *Value Analysis, eco-design* and *Customer Perceived Value*
- Resulting from industrial processes improved by *Lean manufacturing*,
- Supported by governance including *Sustainable Development, Management by Values, Corporate Social Responsibility* or *Shared Value*
- Driven by a *Balanced ScoreCard*,
- Developed using a *V3 - vision, values and will* modeling of the company,
- Organized by *process management*,
- Optimized by *Lean management*,
- Whose information system is adapted to the strategy under the control of *Business Analysts*,
- Where purchases contribute to value creation, through *redesign to cost* and other innovation levers with suppliers, through *Sustainable Purchasing*
- And interpersonal relationships are inspired by Interactive approaches and *Solution Focus coaching*

The deployment of system thinking, through these methods which already exploit it efficiently in many areas of the company, certainly opens considerable hopes for all those who dream of finding in the economy meaning and human.

We note that some of these methods (lean, redesign to cost, value analysis ...) have been deployed in companies with impressive short-term effectiveness, but with deplorable social and environmental consequences and even long-term economic consequences!? Like any tool, a method can be misused ... But - again - do not throw the baby with the bath water? It seems essential to note that these approaches invite (obligate?) To formalize the expectations of the stakeholders: employee, user, supplier ... and are only effective when they are really listened to. We can therefore divert these methods Value(s) from their basic concepts, but this diversion will be at least conscious! The other methods do not take this a priori ... We have regularly observed that the use of these approaches modifies the culture of the teams and the managers of the companies, which then develop a more systemic vision where the internal and external actors are interdependent and Therefore more respectful of each other. So be careful not to limit the transmission of these methods to tools, without insisting on the state of mind that has underpinned them!

Part 3 - Applications of Value(s) thinking

The following pages describe examples of how Value(s) thinking is applied to different areas of the business, and beyond. The aim is to make more explicit the change brought about by these concepts and tools in the resolution of problems of all types. And so demonstrate their relevance to improve collective intelligence.

Let the reader not forget that this is the anonymous account of real projects, which therefore necessarily biased and limited! You will have understood that our Value(s) approach places each project in its own environment and involves stakeholders most directly, which leads each project to a different outcome. The results presented here are therefore not to reproduce as they are, being valid only in the case treated!

The specialists of each domain will certainly find it to repeat ... I invite them however to test Value(s) thinking: it can change a lot! The fourth part deals with the possible synergies between Value(s) thinking and the methods already used in these different fields.

3.1 Application to a business

The goal of a business is commonly defined as "creating wealth", where in capitalism the first beneficiaries are the shareholders. This is obviously not wrong, but many employees, managers and even shareholders do not see this as a motivating goal and are looking for more meaning and purpose in companies!

Applying the value/system approach allows to build a more fulfilling vision of a company:

Needs: What is it for?

Define relations between elements of the environment:

Le Moigne presents any system as a set of elements in relation to a common purpose, relating to elements of the system's environment. The purpose of the elements of a system is to manage relationships between elements outside the system.

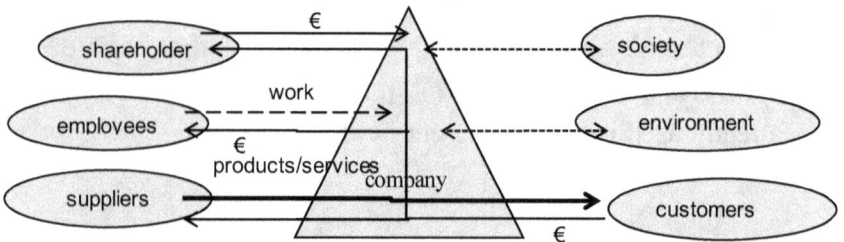

He models a company as a system in direct contact with external entities: shareholders, clients, employees, suppliers, administration, environment and society (its 'stakeholders')

The company manages and transforms flows between these stakeholders: money, products and services, information, energy ...

« For whom? » : Define usefulness for stakeholders

System modeling allows to complete and precise the performances required for the company, its purpose: every company is built to generate value for each of its stakeholders, through what is exchanged with them:

- For shareholders: a financial value, where they will get more money from the company that they put initially, but often also a benefit from participation to decisions or to a global project
- For customers: a use value, where products and services received have more usefulness that what they cost them in money, but also time to access, etc.
- For suppliers: an economic value, where the price received overcomes the resources they put in their realization, but where they may also get visibility on their future, validation on their strategy, etc.
- For employees (which are not part of the company, but are linked to it by a contract and their 'engagement'): an economical value, where salary

balances the time, energy and skills invested, but they also receive a social status, work conditions, improved employability, social interactions, respect for their personal values...
- For the environment: a respectful impact (no pollution) is supposed to balance the resources (air, water ...) and life conditions it 'freely' supplies
- For society (government, NGOs, local authorities and public...): a respect of community rules, minorities, local industrial network, etc. must balance the infrastructures and services it supplies (roads, schools...), as well as the image it vehicles of the company.

It is easy to see that the value perceived by each stakeholder from their exchange with the company is very different, is not always/only measured in economic terms, and can even be subjective or irrational! We should therefore talk about the company value(s), the explicit management of which could provide meaning for the company stakeholders! This finding is not a political or economical a priori, but a direct consequence of the rational use of system modeling.

We also note that each exchange generates value for both parties! For example, the client receives a service that is more useful to him than the agent he cedes, whereas the company finds more use to the money received than the service delivered ... The relative position of each actor makes That all exchanges with the company are win-win, otherwise they do not happen.

When modeling what happens further from the elements in direct contact with the company, we show its insertion into a more global ecosystem:

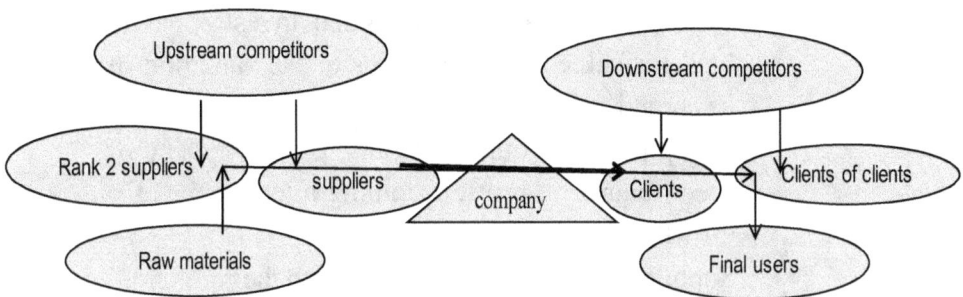

The company's products/services, outputs from successive transformations from raw materials, are often inputs of its clients' own products/services, which will find their real use only during final consumption by final users.

At that level of modeling only appear competitors, which may take clients and suppliers away from the company.

The company strategy should require detailing the levels of performance to be achieved through the exchanges with the company stakeholders, taking into account their own stakeholders needs and requirements.

These strategic requirements cannot be defined correctly without a constructive dialog with each stakeholder, which may reveal specific needs, e.g.:

- A specific shareholder would look for rapid return through dividends, while another for a medium-term increase in the share price on the stock exchange, and another industrial investor would look for value chain synergies or the valuation of its brand on a new market. Instead a 'social entrepreneur' would first target employment of specific groups, profit becoming a 'constraint' for growth.
- Suppliers segmentation according to their potential impact on the company competitiveness, medium and long-term suppliers' strategies, interest to keep suppliers' innovation only for the company… would lead to very different relations and processes

It becomes then obvious that the long-term satisfaction of each stakeholder is depending on the satisfaction of the other company stakeholders: no long-term profit without enthusiastic customers, motivated employees, stable suppliers, respected environment… Any company appears as a system, managing exchanges between interdependent external elements. Many experts consider that each company determines a priority between its stakeholders, leading to define 'one goal' for the company, aiming at satisfying this particular stakeholder: this is at the root of many debates around the importance of shareholders, clients, employees... Even if one category of stakeholders is considered as a priority, his satisfaction becoming THE goal of the company, a system view of the company underlines the interdependency between all stakeholders. Even if ONE ultimate goal is set, it could not be achieved (in the long term) without achieving the other objectives, satisfying the other stakeholders. For example, a public-owned company will target shareholder revenue, but has to take care of clients, and even employees and suppliers. A social entrepreneur will target employment as a goal, but has to generate profit for its investors, to be able to invest for durability and competitiveness!

The prominence of a certain class of stakeholders is 'only' a strategic choice: shares revenues will be preferred in a capitalistic company, while employees' skills development will be preferred by a social enterprise, and another specific objective in a not-for-profit... Every one of them has anyway to secure its economic survival if not growth, and to insure the long-term satisfaction of its stakeholders.

System modeling goes along the most recent theories of the firm: 'stakeholders' theory'11 and 'contracts theory',

---

[11] Freeman, R. Edward (1984). Strategic Management: A stakeholder approach. Boston: Pitman. ISBN 0-273-01913-9.

and offer them a solid scientific background, validated from the latest scientific theories enlarging thinking from 'deterministic' to 'system'.

Stakeholder requirements can be expressed by modeling their relationships with their own environment: upstream and downstream industrial sectors, direct and indirect competitors... to be expressed in terms of purpose, usefulness, and flows transformation.

"When?": Express stakeholders needs at every life cycle step

By analyzing the company life cycle, from its creation to its end, we see that their stakeholder and what performances they require from the company do significantly change: for example (not exhaustive)

- At the company creation:
    - Materialize the project of the will-be entrepreneur: an idea, a specific skill to implement, a lust for autonomy...
    - Multiply the money 'bet' with high risk by initial investors on the will-be entrepreneur project
    - ...
- When activity starts :
    - Develop the company products market and/or market share
    - ...

- At stabilized regime :
    - ➢ Long term :
        - Secure investors return on investment
        - Develop future offers for potential clients with potential customers
        - Secure future capability from potential suppliers
        - …
    - ➢ Mid term :
        - Secure availability of required skills
        - Improve price competitiveness of products with actual suppliers
        - Adapt production tools and processes to required improvements of products performances and costs
        - Develop products visibility for the potential clients
        - …
    - ➢ Short term :
        - Secure actual clients' satisfaction with quality, delays and costs compliant with the promises made
        - Manufacture required products from actual suppliers offers and employees skills

- Manage financial flows from clients to suppliers and employees
- Manage natural, human, political … hazards
- …

- End of life :
  - Secure transmission of accumulated capitals (financial, physical, employees' skills, clients and suppliers relationship …)
  - …

Ressources : What is it for ?

Value = perceived utility(ies) / perceived costs

The company not only has to answer different requirements for its stakeholders but has to do it in way they perceive a positive value in their exchanges with the company: each of them has to think he gets more than he gives! A client will get a product/service where he perceives more usefulness that the price and the time its costs to get it. In the same exchange, the company has to find more usefulness in the money received than to the goods/services delivered! In the same way, thanks to the dissymmetry of their situations, each exchange between the company and its stakeholders has to create value: each one receives more than he gives. Each company definitely is creating value(s)!

Of course, the company will be looking to maximize this value creation, either by improving the perceived usefulness for stakeholders, or reducing their costs, linked to the resources implemented to transform the concerned flows.

Relations between system components

It is possible to model in the same 'system' way the participation of a company components to each flow managed, by visualizing which services and actors manage these flows:

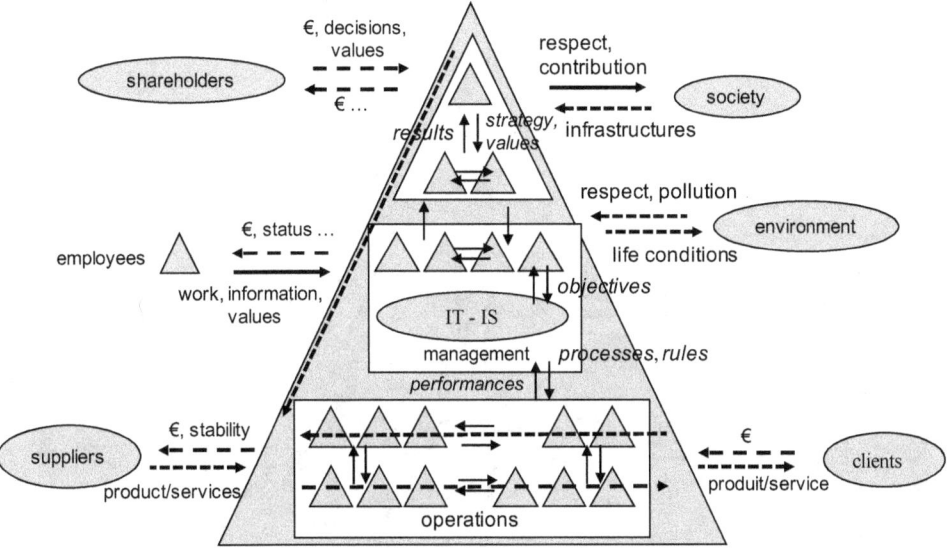

(Adapted from « La théorie du système général. Théorie de la modélisation », 1977, PUF. Reedited in 1986, 1990, 1994 and 2006 as an e-book)

This system modeling allows formalizing the process implemented by a company to manage each of the flows generated by and to its stakeholders. These flows are managed by sequences of operations that most often cross different 'functions' in the company. The interfaces between functions generate risks of lower performance. This modeling show the interest of managing these trans functional processes globally, from stakeholders upstream (e.g. suppliers) to others stakeholders downstream (e.g. clients): a 'management by processes' to be piloted with KPIs defined with the relevant stakeholders.

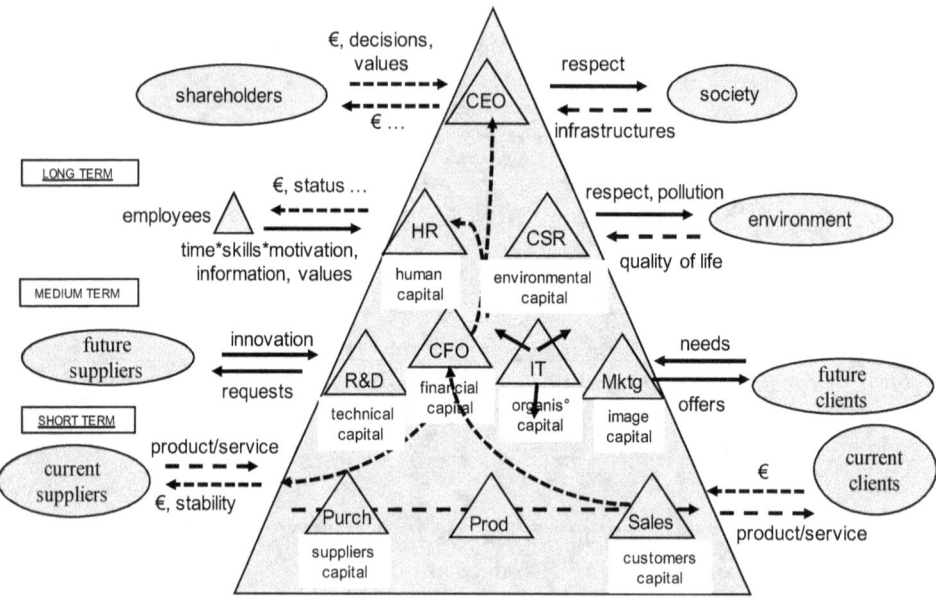

The different *'functions'* in the company specialize in 'creating value' for their own internal and external stakeholders:

- in the short term, Purchasing manages material and subcontracting flows from Actual Suppliers towards Employees and Production, as well as money flowing from Finance (coming from Actual Clients) towards Actual Suppliers ; in medium term, they manage information flows between RD (needs) and Potential suppliers (offers), and Finance (improved costs and cash …) ; in the long term, they manage information flows between Potential Suppliers and CSR (respect of environment and society) and Direction (partnerships, make or buy …), while improving the 'suppliers capital' ;
- IT manages information collection, security, treatment and availability of information between the company functions and external stakeholders, while contributing to increasing its 'organizational capital' ;
- …

We'll present later how to use the same 'system modeling' approach to optimize these processes themselves, and how to 'zoom' on smaller company parts –business units, functions, services- to optimize their local performance while contributing to the global company value creation.

Let us take note that each of the flows managed and transformed by the company between stakeholders leads to an accumulation that constitute a form of 'capital', insuring long term competitiveness to the company and should be closely managed:

- The *financial capital* is the stock of money accumulated by the company, from investors' initial inputs and regular clients' payments, before it is used to pay suppliers and employees or reimburse investors. Part of this capital is necessary to cope with the dis-synchronization of between clients' inputs and suppliers' outputs, to with hazards in futures operations and to reinvest in required skills and tools. The accumulated surplus profit is often considered as the priority objective of the company and the object of all attentions of managers.
- The *physical* capital is made of tools, buildings ... also considered as a priority, but its financial measurement often gives a limited vision of its real usefulness: it should also be measured in terms of obsolescence.
- *Technological* capital consists of machines, but also product and process design through the company's intellectual property, as well as that captured by suppliers.
- Skills accumulated by employees may also be considered as a *human* capital (or resources or,

even better, wealth), from which the usefulness should be related to the actual and future needs of the company, and of its stakeholders: the employees. Too many companies have suffered of not managing the loss of skills linked to retiring or licensing, even at very operational levels. Employees' wellbeing is increasingly recognized as a source of engagement and productivity, therefore competitiveness.
- Other information flows also create *immaterial* capitals which should be later useful to the company and its stakeholders: actual and potential clients information are today the subject to careful consideration; the quality of relations with strategic suppliers has recently been pointed out by Prof. John Henke as of strategic importance.
- Even the *environmental* capital and the *reputation* capital of a company (and its brands) appear decisive for a company's future.

It may be difficult to measure these different capitals in economic or financial terms, but it is relatively easy to measure each of them in its own terms, by indicators relative to the flow they manage, according to the levels where they are considered useful by the relevant company stakeholders: turnover and employability of/for employees, quality of relations, participation to innovation and stability of/for suppliers …

This model can be used to redefine any organization's strategy, to build a new business model, target new potential markets, design synergies across the value chain ...

"What is enough?"

Creating value(s) for each stakeholder

The 'system' vision of the company and its components allows to (re)define its strategy as 'generate which value for which stakeholders'!

Of course, some may be prioritized by certain categories of firms: shareholders for stock market corporations, employees for a social enterprise ... But none of them can be neglected on the long term! Exploring their respective needs has to be done by listening to their own values. The company results will then be measured with indicators of stakeholder needs satisfaction from their exchanges with the company: these are not all being finance-driven, eg. employees' wellbeing, suppliers' engagement, ...

Creating value(s) by useful transformation flows

The company can be modelled as a set of processes transforming upstream stakeholders' inputs (suppliers' goods, employees work, shareholders money...) into downstream stakeholders' outputs (clients services, employees salary, suppliers money...). These material, financial, information flows can be optimized by avoiding spending resources that do not contribute to downstream stakeholders' satisfaction.

Manage short, medium and long-term processes separately

Stakeholders have different horizons for their needs: e.g. shareholders want dividends in the long term compared to suppliers and employees. Each function in the company has then to manage different processes with different skills:

- Short term = Operations: create value for customers
    - Manage material, energy, subcontracting … flows from suppliers, transformed by employees into products/services,
    - Manage money flow from customers towards employees, suppliers …
    - Target short term stakeholders performance: suppliers' compliance with Quality, Delays and Costs; customers QCD satisfaction; …
    - Functions involved: procurement > manufacturing > sales > supply chain > billing
- Medium term = Management: adapt Operations contribution to current stakeholders' satisfaction

- - o Manage information flows about satisfaction and evolutions of actual stakeholders needs
  - o Target medium term performance: react to QCD failures and improve value creation for current company stakeholders
  - o Functions involved: purchasing > quality > operational marketing > operational HR > supply chain > accounting
- Long term = Strategy: adapt to future stakeholders and needs evolutions
  - o Manage information flows about long term evolutions and environment of current company stakeholders, e.g. stakeholders' own stakeholders (competitors, other value chain actors …) or future potential stakeholders (market segments not yet targeted, potential suppliers …)
  - o Target long term performance: improve value proposition on QCD, react to stakeholders' risks, target new stakeholders and needs
  - o Involved functions: upstream purchasing > R&D > engineering > strategic marketing > finance

Innovation is not a goal!

Innovation, whether limited to research, technological aspects or extended to all improvements in the supply or the means of the company, is considered as one of the most important processes, guaranteeing its competitiveness in the Time, and to which all should devote important means.

But what is the innovation process, if not all the means that help to adapt the processes and the company's offer to the evolutions of its stakeholders: the needs of the customers, the resources of its suppliers and partners? Innovation is not an end in itself: its value is to develop the creation of future value by improving operations, for current or future stakeholders.

It can be understood that innovation can only be a matter of scientists enclosed in their R & D, or of marketers turned to the emotions of their clients: the identification of the evolutions of the stakeholders should be the responsibility of those who are already at their Contact: sellers, buyers, after-sales service ...! And that the sources of inspiration on other ways of meeting these needs are obviously not only inside the company but outside, and that the majority of innovations should come from the integration by the " Company of solutions already existing elsewhere, ideally not in the same competitive sector.

Managers, what are they for?

The part of the company that is directly useful to customers and other stakeholders is that which transforms the inputs of suppliers and other partners into products / services for customers: the operational ones. Support functions are used to adapt products and resources to short- and long-term stakeholder developments. But what is the use of managers: middle management, functional managers ...? This role comes from a hierarchical vision of the company, where only executives are supposed to have a complete vision of the company and its destinies. The system vision of the company puts this role in question: the operational ones in contact with the stakeholders are the best to perceive the satisfaction and evolutions of their needs? There is no need for managers to steer ... It remains an interface between the players in the value chain, the dissemination of developments perceived on the ground, coordination with support functions, transfer of skills to operational staff: A top-down distribution belt as a coach and catalyst. This role can be held outside the hierarchy.

This role corresponds to the control of the feedback loops of the system approach: once the ways of meeting the needs of the stakeholders and the operational processes to realize them are established, it remains to be checked continuously whether these must be adapted:

a. Internal loop: do business processes do what is expected? It is the quality and lean spirit, which can be achieved by the actors themselves
b. Existing external loop: Are current stakeholders well satisfied with the outputs of the company's processes: it is one of the roles of marketing and customer-side quality, Supplier-side procurement, HR (human resources) Side employees ...
c. Future external loop: Future evolutions of stakeholder needs or the emergence of new stakeholders are identified to prepare new ways to serve them: it is the role of Strategic Marketing, Upstream Purchasing, Strategy ...

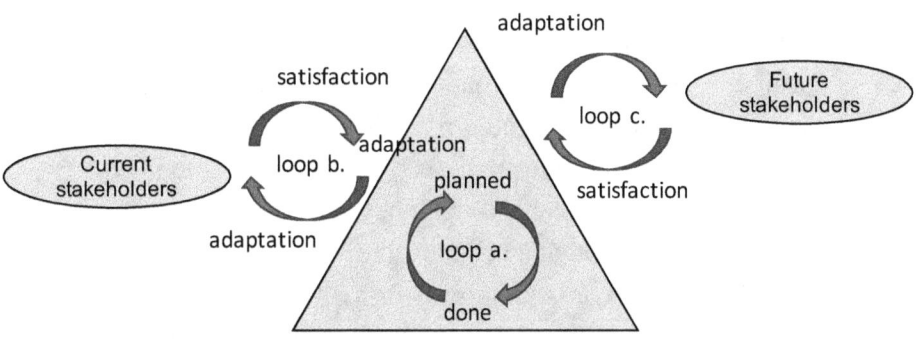

Systems theory -and our common sense- tells us that these loops must be the shortest and most reactive possible: when you approach the hand of a flame, the reflex arc which causes the hand to withdraw does not pass through consciousness ("It's too hot, I have to pull my hand out") and not even by the brain! It is managed by the spinal cord, decision center much closer to the sensation and the muscles that must react.

Feedback loops may be negative, such as in a thermostat that cuts off the heating when the desired temperature is reached, or positive, such as reinvesting interest earned on an investment. A great advantage is the setting up of positive feedback loops: for example, highlighting customer satisfaction on social networks will snowball (be careful to avoid making negative feedback loop ...)

Improving a company's market value

A manager was mandated by the Board of his company, a national fast food chain, to implement a diversification project. After some years of success, the initial shareholders were secretly preparing the selling of the company to its highest possible stock market value. They built up a strategic plan to create new revenue streams just before the sale, so that a brighter future would increase the bride's attractiveness. The project manager and its team selected a new product line to be launched: besides the current hot sandwiches offer, they would also sell a cold sandwiches line. Profitability was ok, the market was ready, restaurants were adaptable ... so everything looked perfect! Before implementation, they hired a Value(s) expert for a final check.

The first question was of course "What is it for?". The company Board answers were: the cold sandwiches are to be sold to new customers, to make more profit, to increase the share value of the company, to make more money for its future shareholders ... so that the company will be sold at a higher price by the actual stakeholders.

Makes sense? But a crucial point is missed: "work WITH the stakeholders"!

In this case, who are we working for, but the future shareholders? Of course, it is difficult to work with them directly when secretly preparing the sale! But the expert insisted on defining who these future shareholders could be and the manager made the Board list the different options: either a financial investor or a company in the same fast food sector willing to make an industrial and/or commercial synergy.

"What is enough for them?" Of course, a profitable investment ... but each would have its own criteria: many investors want to secure profits more than put money in a risky venture? Another hot fast food chain would probably be interested in enlarging its commercial footprint for its own product line? A 'cold' sandwiches chain would be interested in synergy between product lines?

Who would really be interested in the planned diversification to cold sandwiches? Nobody else than ... the actual shareholders! So, the project was abandoned.

Building the business model of a social entrepreneur

A senior manager in a major electric appliances company decided to "change the world" and launch a startup in the recycling industry: many people buy new appliances while the previous is still ok, which goes into a storage closet. And secondhand shops lack attractive items, because those collected often come from waste collection sites and are spoiled or broken in the process.

So, he planned to launch a company targeting the selling on the internet of guaranteed quality second hand appliances, by collecting them 'at the source' during events organized by large companies CSR managers for their employees.

This project pleased many people, but was difficult to launch: the investment to build the required e-commerce website is significant, the time needed for the development of the app was too long for our new entrepreneur, the catalog of appliances has to be wide to attract web clients … and eBay did not wait for him to offer the same items.

We organized a Value(s) thinking evening, that delivered the following ideas:

"Work with the stakeholders" led to invite e-commerce specialists and recycling experts, but also CSR managers and … people like me and you.

Asking them "What is it for you?" underlined very specific requirement at each step of the Value(s) chain:

- CSR managers need to promote their company image to their employees;
- Employees are glad to free space at home while contributing to positive social and environmental impacts;
- Recyclers need a not spoiled source of items and a distribution channel for their recycled goods;
- Internet buyers need bargains but guaranteed refurbished quality appliances.

This led the startup's initial business model to be reversed and cut in 3 'agile' stages:

1. An 'event' company selling its 'collect days' services to CSR managers, without any investment, to be launched immediately in partnership with recyclers. The goods would be sold through the recyclers shops ... and eBay!
2. A marketing consulting company helping recyclers upgrade their communication with quality pictures, 'quality refurbish' guarantee ...
3. A dedicated e-commerce platform would be developed in a later stage, with the money collected from the first business stages, if still necessary after the Marketing improvements?

3.2 Application to a production unit

Take the example of a (real) project to improve the competitiveness of a business unit for manufacturing and distribution of bottled spring water in an Eastern European country, for a subsidiary of an international group whose management must restore profitability: the local brand does not allow the premium prices of its competitors. A project to improve industrial profitability is therefore launched according to our approach.

Needs: What is it for?

The utility of the BU, spontaneously expressed by its managers, is to "create wealth" by offering on the market (2 distinct geographic regions) products (bottles of water) that meet the needs of its customers better than its competitors. One finds the difficulty of defining only one goal? We have here two distinct levels:

- transforming source water into profit for the group (the 'raison d'être' of the BU for the industrial group)

- transforming spring water into bottles of water on the market (the raison d'être of the BU for its customers)

The two goals cohabit but are dependent: by (re) asking the question " what is it for? for each of these, we see that the initial goal is that of the industrial group, which has chosen to distribute bottled water on the market as a means of creating wealth. Bottled water, and the market pays for bottles to generate profit for the group.

The relations between elements:

The system modeling allows us to specify the relations and flows of the BU with the elements of its environment:

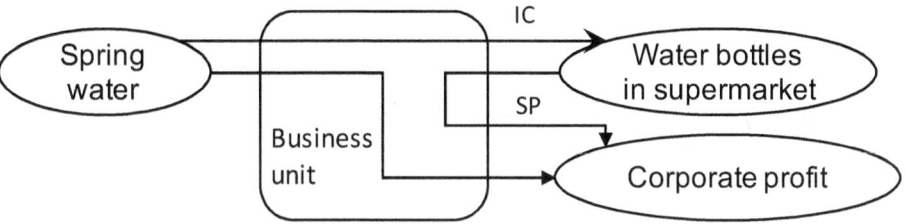

The objective of improving competitiveness can therefore be achieved in two ways:

- reduce the industrial cost (IC)
- or increase the selling price (SP)

The analysis with the teams shows that the reduction of costs is not easy, the means of the BU being difficult to challenge:

- the machines of the two factories, located in the mountains, one near the capital and the other of the tourist areas of the South of the country, are already cushioned,

- plastic is bought at group level from global suppliers,
- energy is provided by the state,
- the labor force is inexpensive and the teams very limited ... even if the wages are higher in the oldest of the factories, by effect of seniority
- remain the labels and the transport, whose optimization does not make it possible to reach the objective.

Can we increase the selling price? Analyze the needs of the product and whether it can be improved

"When?": Life cycle stages

The life cycle of the water bottle includes several steps:

- before use: manufacture of the bottle, filling, transport to the distributor, sale to the consumer, transport to the home, preservation
- in use: for drinking or cooking (capital cooks do not use tap water, bad taste in this country)
- after use: storage between 2 uses, empty bottle removed

The system approach emphasizes the most direct involvement of stakeholders: consumers, distributors, manufacturers, suppliers, etc. The exploration of needs and solutions makes it possible to imagine improvements with them:

- marketing highlights two different types of use: drinking water, consumed glass by glass and fresh (taken from the fridge) and cooking water, used by 1 liter at a time, at room temperature. The current solution, the pack of 6 bottles of 1,5 liter sold at the local store, serves both needs.
- some cooks prefer the 8 liters bottle for cooking, but they are too heavy and more often bought in department store and brought back by car. Improvements would be possible (home delivery, ...) but proved to be too expensive.

Since the improvement in the selling price is difficult, how to reduce the cost? The question will be to verify that the resources implemented in water bottles are very useful and necessary and sufficient?

Resources: What is it for?

The system modeling makes it possible to highlight different utilities for the components:

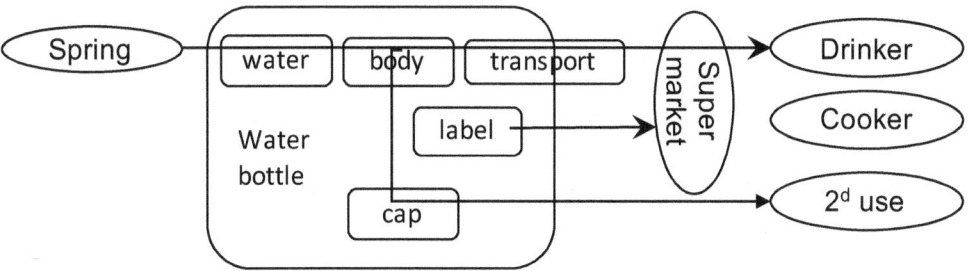

What answers consumers' needs is:

- **water** (!), For the different uses of drinks and cooking.

We note with surprise that its cost is ... no! Indeed, the industrialist obtained the concession of the source for free. But not for nothing: the installation of the factory in the mountain provided labor and local taxes!

So nothing to optimize ... And besides, why is the customer willing to pay for this free resource? To be able to benefit from it where it is ...

- its **transport** from the source,

This represents 20% of the cost, in pallets and subcontracting to the premises that bought trucks during the construction of the plant. This cost is useful, since the source is not where the drinker is. Can we limit this cost? Of course, local truckers can compete with other logistics professionals who can be more efficient. The option was quickly dismissed: the impact on the local economy would be too great, and mountain roads soon become much less safe ...

No significant optimization possible for transport.

- the **body** of the bottle which allows it to be sold in quantities of 1,5 l

This represents 80% of the cost: plastic, forming machines, energy, labor, ... This cost is a priori useful: without bottle how to transport water? Other solutions exist: a pipeline (too expensive and impractical from a distance), tank trucks (water should be delivered to customers' containers, recycled bottles, or bottled on the spot ... no options viable).

Can we limit this cost? Are the 15 grams of plastic shaped bottle necessary and sufficient? A quick search highlights another solution: a bag of 3-4g of plastic is enough to carry 1.5 water! This solution exists for humanitarian needs, refills of cosmetic products ... Why not for water? In fact, the 15g plastic also serve other purposes:

> Hold the water on the table and in a glass

Everyone knows the low-cost bottles that crash when you handle them and do not stand up. But what about the use in the kitchen, where all the contents are poured into a pan?! The bag is enough. And for the drink, you could just pour the water transported in a bag in ... a carafe?

> Open and close after use

The **neck** of the body, on which the cap is screwed, weighs 15% of the body. They are useful for drinking water, but what about cooking water?! To open, the bag and a pair of scissors, already in the kitchen, are enough. And no need to close! And for the drinking water transported in a minimal bag, the closing can be carried out with a simple pinch. Or to provide a resealable carafe?

- the **label** serves the distributor, to present the mark, and the legal indications

On a premium bottle, enhancing the brand is useful, but on a low-cost brand, you just need to be able to read the directions. If it is difficult to print directly on a shaping bottle, no problem to do it on a plastic bag, printed flat before filling!

- the **cap**, and the part of the bottle to screw it (1 / 5th of the plastic) serves in case the use is done in several times and you want to conserve water in the shelter.

It has been seen above that the plug is connected to the neck of the body. It is only useful for drinking water and not for cooking.

What is enough?

From this analysis, the solution can be considerably simplified for cooks: replace 15g of plastic in place and the paper label with a pre-printed bag. The impact of this radical innovation on the subsidiary's business model is considerable: replacing existing plants, in fact plastic bottle manufacturing plants, by filling preformed, much simpler bags. This can also be envisaged much closer to the distribution zones, from tankers coming from the mountains. We understand that this change is not easy for a company already in place ...

The fine analysis also makes it possible to consider improvements for drinking water:

> Offer lighter bottles of 5l, to be placed flat in the fridge, closed by a sealed cover with a faucet sold separately (not offered with each bottle)

> Propose a home delivery service, which may include a social dimension through the employment of people in difficulty returning to work

> Also propose the recovery of empty packaging, for better recycling: the positive impact on the environment is cumulated with an economic impact, the plastic to be recycled being no longer mixed with other waste, should no longer be cleaned or sorted

These services are more or less valued by different types of users:

- wealthy customers will agree to pay more for an easy-to-use fresh water supply,
- older people will agree to pay for a delivery in the floors,
- ecological customers will agree to contribute to recycling, which then allows to resell the material or reuse it and thus limit costs ...

For single use, small bottles with a non-closable lid, compatible with sports accessories, will be offered: insulated protection, straw for drinking current, carrying strap ...

Pending the implementation of these radical innovations, many optimizations have been made possible:

\> Reduce the height of the screw of the neck and the cap

\> Reduce the surface of the label, make plastic, glue them cold and not hot

\> Allow 6 bottles to be transported with a single finer film, instead of a thick film plus a carton

\> The price of the transport being included in the fixed price of the delivered bottles, do not deliver the distributors beyond a distance which makes the sale in deficit, or make pay the transport according to the distance

The modeling system thus facilitates innovation in the optimization of the business model, by highlighting:

- the usefulness of the product manufactured and the services to be attached thereto,
- the segmentation of the market between types of use,
- the possible revenue stream, linked to the perceived value of each service to be rendered by

those to whom it generates income or avoids costs or inconveniences,
- the impact of location on profitability,
- the importance of activity on the territory and the local economy,
- different roles played by the components of a product yet simple,
- radically different solutions to meet the needs ...

3.3 Application to a business function: Purchasing

Take the example of Purchasing: a specific service of the organization or function of the company historically dedicated to contacts with suppliers, from their selection to the day-to-day acquisition of the supplies needed to manufacture the products and services offered by the business and means of operation of all functions.

Needs: What is it for?

The relations between elements:

The system modeling of the Purchasing function can be done by formalizing its relations with its stakeholders: suppliers (current and potential, also stakeholders of the company), production, finance, R & D, etc. Internal to the company, themselves in relation with other external stakeholders of the company.

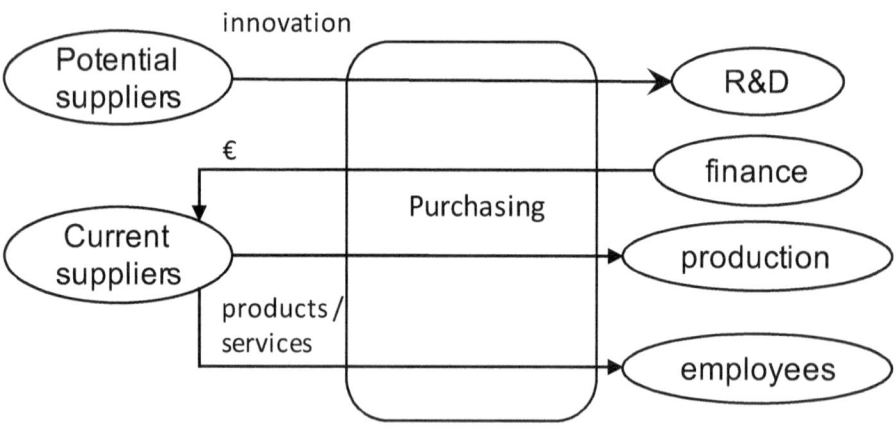

"Who is it for? ": for stakeholders

The performance expectations of these stakeholders are different: attention will be paid to a careful dialogue to understand and formalize these expectations.

Different suppliers in the same sector, depending on their shareholding, competitive positioning, technological development capacity and geographical location, will attach different importance to the stability of their relationship with the company, its support for international development and even Price offered by the company!

Knowledge of the real expectations of internal stakeholders - that is, the construction of offers that meet the expectations of future customers - is not at all obvious to buyers, and the legitimacy they can obtain from their Many R & D managers consider that a buyer can not bring value to an innovation process, whereas suppliers are often a very relevant source of innovation and a necessary passage for innovation, industrialization!

"When?" ": Life cycle stages

By analyzing the relationships managed by purchases, we find that their relationships with stakeholders do not have the same time scale, and that other performances are expected at specific times.

Purchasing brings value to multiple stakeholders across different time horizons by not only economic exchange:

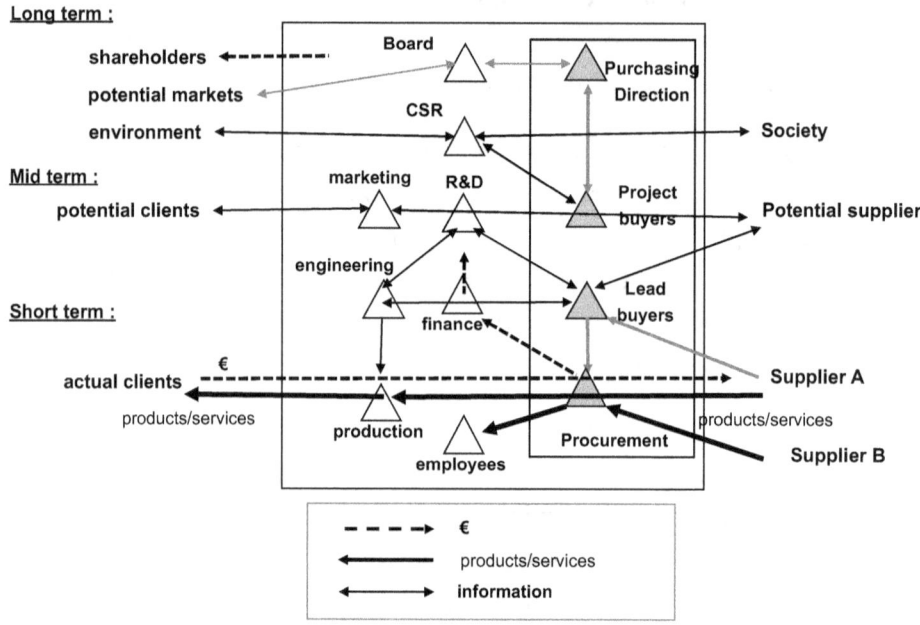

In the short term (operations), supplies bring value:

- to manufacturing (and then to customers): to make available the products / services of the suppliers, with indicators Quality / Costs / Delays; Avoid environmental impacts; Improving working conditions
- to manufacturing (and then to customers): to make available the products / services of the suppliers,

with indicators Quality / Costs / Delays; Avoid environmental impacts; Improving working condition
- to suppliers: to pay the sums due in exchange for the services

In the medium term (leadership), the buyers' buyers / buyers family bring:

- potential suppliers, opportunities and visibility on their activities
- engineering, questioning of needs and solutions, supplier QCD risk analyzes
- approvals, expertise, framework contracts and negotiating support
- to finance, the achievement of the full cost objectives
- management, and control of the risks incurred

In the long run (strategy), upstream purchases provide;

- R & D supplier innovations and the feasibility of new products
- to the CSR manager, information on respect for the environment and Corporate Social Responsibility: territorial impact, working conditions ...
- to suppliers, strategic collaborations
- management, validation of the industrial feasibility of the strategy through innovation with suppliers, integration or subcontracting of operations with

suppliers, control of the company extended to its value chain at worldwide
- Purchasing employees, improving their welfare (pride?) At work and their employability
- capital accumulated in the company: material (financial, physical, technological) and intangible (human, customer relations and suppliers, environmental, image ...)

Resources: What is it for?

Each stakeholder must perceive a positive value (utility / cost) in its exchanges with the Purchases: the exchange must be positive for each of the parties, in a win/win relationship! It is therefore essential for purchasing companies to measure the satisfaction of their stakeholders, both internally and externally. The indicators of this satisfaction can be global, as many companies implement them in processes where the functions are inscribed in internal customer / supplier relationships or more precise, such as the quality indices of the supplier relationship proposed by the Professor John Henke, or indicators of supplier participation in innovation, CSR indicators, etc.

Purchasing can also assess their satisfaction with the inputs of upstream functions in the process: for example, the quality of specifications which largely determines the effectiveness of purchases in providing an optimal supplier solution, Buyers to select a new supplier, opening to proposals facilitating purchasing groupings, ...

The costs of the company are of course linked to the effectiveness of the Purchases: indicators are now systematic for the regular monitoring of their effectiveness in reducing costs. But it is more difficult to establish the impact of purchasers on the reduction of quantities consumed or on the adjustment of a level of performance ... More qualitative indicators are essential to assess the value of purchases in other Terms that are purely economic, even quantitative: a good score of satisfaction of the Production with regard to the quality and the delays of supply can have much more value than a reduction of cost!

Relationship between system components:

It has been observed that purchasing brings different values to different time horizons: the actors, processes and tools needed for procurement and upstream purchases, for example, are quite different. An optimal purchasing organization will carefully distinguish these different levels of the process.

What is enough?

Overall Procurement Role and Performance

A new way of evaluating the performance of purchasing is to be derived from these elements: what value creation (s) for their stakeholders? Their satisfaction can be measured:

- Are purchasers aware of the need to satisfy all their internal stakeholders: purchasing users (production, employees), engineering, finance, R & D, CSR, branch? And that these roles imply different skills (actors?)? (Procurement, category managers, project buyers, upstream purchases, responsible purchasing, purchasing department ...)
- And also to satisfy their external stakeholders: suppliers? (And not just to get the most out of it)
- Do purchases know the expectations of their interlocutors?
- How satisfied are the actors in contact with Purchasing with their relationship?
- Are there indicators, processes, tools to formalize these expectations and measure their satisfaction?
- Is the procurement process managed by Procurement alone, or carried out by a process involving all the actors involved in the design and implementation of the company's products / services?
- How are purchases perceived by management?
    - ➢ an operational actor,
    - ➢ a holder of operating income (costs),
    - ➢ a vector of medium-term competitiveness (profit, innovation, CSR),

> a participant in the company strategy (extended company, integrated supply chain, circular economy, business model shared with suppliers, etc.)

Evaluation can be done with different levels of sophistication:

- a simple 360 ° survey of the satisfaction of the partners, anonymous or not,

- an exhaustive exploration of the impacts of purchases on the performance of each of these interlocutors, for example: number of tracks of innovations made to R & D, level of achievement of the environmental objectives of the CSR Directorate, number of supply disruptions Avoided for production ...

Each of these roles uses different information, at different time horizons, and may need to be held by people with different skills

Progress actions: cost (s) or value (s)?

In concrete terms, this change in the systemic point of view of purchasing leads to the completion of the types of actions entrusted to purchasing: the reduction in purchasing costs is part of it, in order to better satisfy shareholders and / or to offer customers satisfaction for cheaper ...

But buyers are obviously well positioned to generate the resources of current and potential suppliers and improve solutions to better serve customers, internal users and other stakeholders:

> The purchase price is obviously important, but not to the detriment of the quality of the supplies! Redesign-To-Cost targets the best solution at a given price.

> Not at the expense of the relevance of the solution: have potential suppliers proposed the best solutions? Value analysis revisits the design of purchased components, in collaboration with internal product designers - Engineering and R & D - and customers' contact points - Marketing and Marketing.

> The cost price of the company's products / services includes purchases of supplies and subcontracting but also their transformation into the company. Are the solutions of the suppliers the most effective to limit this cost of transformation - energy, labor, machines, transport ... -

> Employee efficiency is also dependent on the quality and comfort of the tools available to them, and even the motivation that their use generates: Indirect purchases are also factors of productivity! The Value(s) reflection must also be carried out on the one hand, Production and Logistics and on the other hand General Services.

> Are innovations on products, related services, the business model of its marketing possible from the solutions developed by suppliers? Will they reserve them for the company or will they share them with competitors? Steps to economize on functionality and circular economy are possible. Procurement will work with Marketing and R & D, but also the CFO to stay one step ahead of future markets.

> Production is constantly looking for ways to improve: how to improve the machines and tools of the processes without suppliers and purchases? The Supplier Development aims to improve its suppliers to remain more competitive.

> Where to install new production capacity for new geographic markets? Doing / doing, buying / renting equipment / services / results ...? These strategic decisions assume a role as purchasing professionals, but the required skills do not necessarily belong to buyers or not to the same roles?

> Production performance is also subject to risks: supply flow breakdown, supplier bankruptcy, currency risk, the image of a failing supplier ... Purchases are now targeting the cost / benefit * risk ratio.

> At a more strategic level, how to extend the control upstream and downstream of their value chain.

Interdependence with suppliers (and distributors) assumes the responsibility of managing the extended enterprise?

> Finance seeks to improve purchasing costs but often neglects to involve purchases in the most important purchases: investments! Nice synergies are possible by applying the Value(s) methods on the CapEx.

> Finance also has other objectives than the expenditure figures: cash, impacted by fixed assets (inventories and investments) and supplier payment periods involve purchases!

> The financial health of suppliers is important for the company, which depends on them (at least some) for its survival and competitiveness.

> Users also incur other expenses to implement the company's product / service: energy, time and labor, etc. It is possible to limit the Total Cost of Ownership, by innovating with suppliers.

> The costs perceived by clients are not only financial: time, effort, environmental impact, social and territorial impact, image, ethics ... can be targets of the efforts of the General Management, which will entrust Responsible Purchasing with the responsibility of mastering The responsibility of suppliers and ideally the reflection on responsible innovation.

Purchasing is perhaps the function of the most advanced company of its evolutions towards the management of the extended and responsible company. But their specifications are getting heavier ... Fortunately, this process is first and foremost a matter of collaboration with the other functions of the company!

3.4 Application to an information process

Let us take the example of a simple tertiary process: the credit agreement to a potential customer in a bank, via a file received in an agency and processed by a centralized service. We are trying to improve it for the bank that is implementing it: either reducing costs or innovating to improve its performance.

Needs: What is it for?

As for an industrial process, direct observation of the process makes it possible to specify its purpose "to give credit" thanks to system modeling, by representation of the relations managed in terms of inputs and outputs:

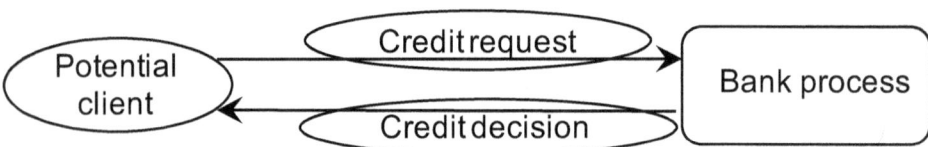

This process allows a bank to transform a credit application from a potential customer into a decision to grant the credit.

The expected performance of this process corresponds to the dimensioning of this relationship: the number of files processed and accepted, speed and quality of decisions (the rate of customer failure).

This will be complemented by the expected performance at each phase of the life cycle: for example,

- before use: setting up the required tools and skills ...

- during: processing incomplete files

- after: changes in regulations ...

Resources: What is it for?

The improvement of the value of this type of process is conventionally aimed at reducing the time consumed, which is the source of both cost and dissatisfaction of customers.

We use the system modeling of the stages of the process, to formalize with the stakeholders (customers, bank branch, headquarters expert ...), or in a graphic form:

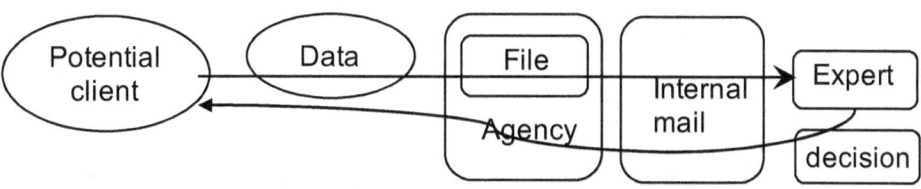

Either in the form of an input / output table:

Step	Input	time	Output
1° application	Agency request	minutes	File to be completed
2° folder	Customer data	days	Completed
3° transfer	Internal shuttle	2 days	File on expert desk
4° wait	Time limit	2-3 days	File in expert hands
5° analysis	Expert Time	1 hour	Decision taken: yes / no / details
6° transfer	Internal shuttle	2 days	Decision to the Agency
7° appointment	Business time	2-3 days	Decision ready to be transmitted
8° customer	Customer Time	minutes	Decision sent to client

Let us note that this process, like many processes of information processing:

- includes only very limited time: here, that of decision-making and its transmission to the client
- generates many temporary outputs, a priori useless, characteristics resulting from a step that will be transformed in the following. These stages are generally born of ends other than the raison d'être of the process:
- reporting to management,
- processing of files by lot,
- registration for further analysis,
- cutting into stages treated by different people,
- ...

They can often be called into question. Here, most of the time is related to transfers - from the file to the expert and from the expert to the agency - and to the availability of the expert. This transfer is due to the scarcity of expertise necessary for decision-making, available only at headquarters. And the time taken is due to the transfer of a file, containing paper elements transmitted by the client (bank statements, tax returns, deposit ...). Should the paper dossier be challenged, or even the necessity of an expert?

What is enough?

These findings, which were classic in many administrative processes, would have led very quickly to the obvious decision to computerize the file. This makes it possible to speed up the flow of files between agency and expert, at a minimal cost in agency, possibly even to entrust the client himself!

System modeling allows us to go further: question the purpose of the information requested from the client for the decision. They serve to reassure the bank about the quality of the borrower's file: will it be able to repay the loan in the conditions allowing the bank to earn money? A search without a priori with bankers, customers, non-bankers ... made it possible to determine the necessary and sufficient information:

- Know the historical behavior of the borrower: the "cicadas" do not become "ants"! The Banque de France has lists of bad borrowers.

- Check whether the borrower has a chronic repayment capacity: stable income exceeding stable expenses. Bank statements are the best source for this type of information.

However, most credit applications are from clients of the bank, which therefore already has sufficient information to determine the quality of the borrower! Why apply for additional income tax returns? For historical reasons: we always did like that. And why even ask at this stage for a surety: the latter is useful only if the bank has granted a credit when it should not have ... or in case of unforeseen event. The guarantor therefore does not enter the decision to grant the credit, but in the fixing of the rate of the loan to cover the risks. It was therefore decided to optimize this process by granting the loans directly to the agency from the account history already held by the bank and the prompt questioning of the Banque de France files.

The advantage of this approach compared to the digitalization seen above is obvious: not only are we avoiding transfers, but we multiply the processing capacity until we propose an almost immediate response to the client. This makes it possible to imagine dealing with more files, if these were requested in larger numbers. The project of a marketing campaign to the clients therefore arose naturally: the bank would be able to respond to its customers to any request for credit. And since it already has the information to decide whether to grant a loan if requested, this bank has analyzed the data of its customers to offer credit to its best customers, even before they ask for it! The gain in value created, both for customers (no more delay) and for bank accounts (maximum file quality) is very significant! And computerization is always possible.

These astonishing observations can only be made by working directly with the stakeholders, the headquarters expert. And the questioning of the current process is impossible without its endorsement: if credit decisions (re) become simple and within the reach of an agency, it loses its status of indispensable expert, even its position! The value / system approach paying attention to people and their values, the question of the finality of the process for the expert himself has been raised: to guarantee him a respectable and useful post. The implementation of the new process has thus easily integrated this objective: the former essential expert has become trainer of the processing agents' simple files and remains the expert called for the atypical requests where his years of experience prove invaluable.

The system modeling thus brings to the tertiary processes the same improvements as for the industrial processes, but especially facilitates the work of questioning an organization by involving the stakeholders - those using the results of the process studied and those involved in their current realization and future - considering their own objectives and needs! This type of project often involves the skills of ergonomists, psychologists, cognitivists, etc. Knowing how to formalize the real needs of people better than themselves. On the other hand, this type of project cannot be used effectively without a state of mind of trust and respect of values ...

3.5 Application to an industrial process

Let us take the example of a simple industrial process: the manufacture of foam breads of car seats. We are trying to improve it for its manufacturer: either reduce costs or innovate to improve performance.

Needs: What is it for?

The utility of the process expressed spontaneously would be to "make foam bread".

The relations between elements:

This is not false, but the system modeling allows us to specify, by direct observation of the process and representation of the relations managed in terms of inputs and outputs:

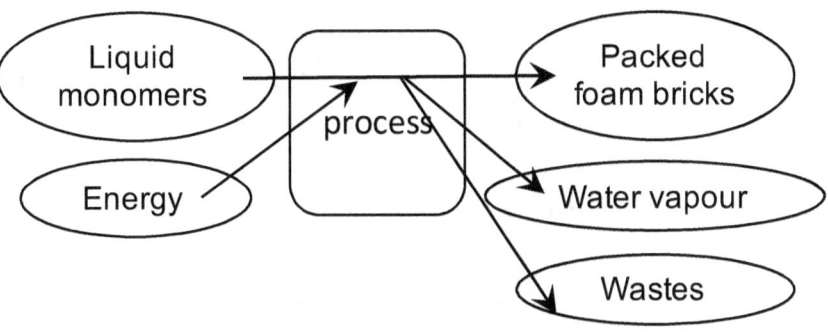

This makes it possible to specify: the process makes it possible to convert liquid monomers and energy into packaged foam cakes, and generates water and scrap.

The interest of these details? The purpose of the process is to produce foam breads, but here we point out all the inputs and outputs of the process, even those not wanted: one might want to make the foam with other monomers, less energy, other tools ... And avoid generating scrap.

The expected performances of the process -its purpose- corresponds to the dimensioning of this relation: the quantities and characteristics of the monomers, energy, tools, foam cakes, water, scrap.

"When?" ": Life cycle stages

By analyzing the relationships managed by the process at each phase of its life cycle, the expected performances are complemented: for example (not exhaustive)

- before use: adapt to the site, building and utilities available
- between 2 uses: facilitating cleaning and maintenance
- after use: facilitate the downstream process
  - seats manufacturing = unpacking / control ...
  - vehicles manufacturing = assembly ...
  - vehicle use = passenger comfort ...
- at the end of life: respecting the environment

"Resources: For what? ": The relations between components

If one wishes to improve the value of this process, one will want either to reduce the cost, to improve the performances, or 2. The system modeling of the process components is done by studying the successive phases of the transformation:

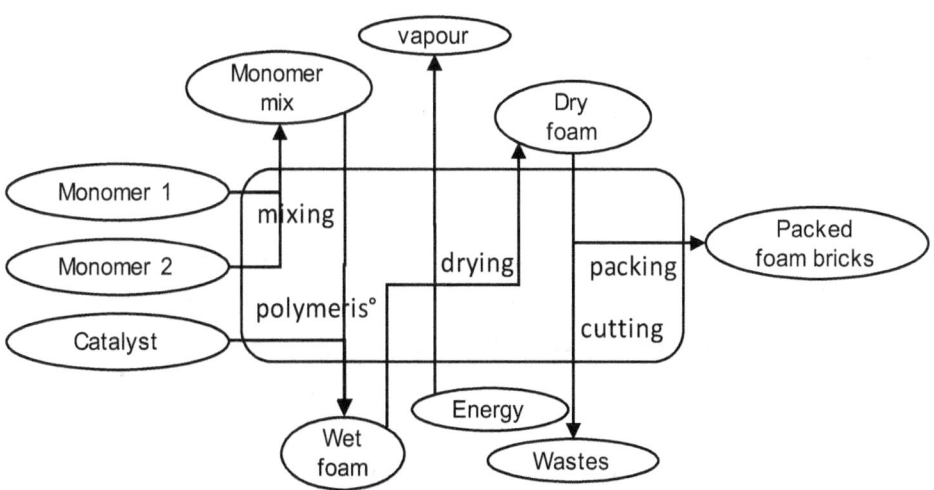

A simpler formalization in a table is possible for the analysis of the process steps:

Step	INPUT	OUTPUT (useful / *not*)
1° mixing	Monomers 1 + 2	*Monomers mix*
2° polymerisation	Catalyst + time	*Wet* polymer *block*
3° drying	Energy	*Block* of dry polymer + *vapour*
4° cutting	Tool	Foam blocks + *wastes*
5° packaging	Packaging + manpower	Packed *foam blocks*

We note that this process - like all others - generates outputs of 2 types: definitive or temporary. For the latter, the acquired characteristics will be transformed again, and these steps are thus a priori useless (in italics in the table above). They are easy to spot thanks to system modeling: the useful characteristics of the process are not present upstream and must be present downstream.

What is enough?

How to improve process performance? By improving the quality or quantity of outputs produced, here packaged foam bread.

How to reduce the cost of the process from this system modeling? By limiting the necessary inputs: line, energy, tool, packaging. Or by avoiding producing unnecessary outputs: the only one corresponding to the raison d'être of the process is the last one, the dry foam bread packed; The others are not indispensable: water and scrap, or are temporary: the wet foam, the block of foam unpacked.

As for the products, the systematic search for the simplest means to satisfy the utilities of the process opens paths of innovation:

The designer may choose other polymers to produce the foam, for example with a reaction that does not produce water and avoids drying,

- Or directly produce the final size bread, avoiding the cutting

To improve performance, the relationship between the system and the stakeholders is sought. Exploring their needs will make it possible to imagine improvements.

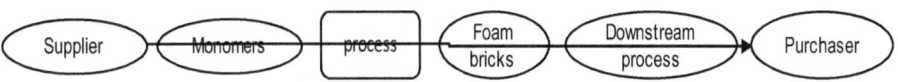

Here, the stakeholders are first the manufacturer and the buyer of foam breads. The need to satisfy is to provide the buyer with the desired foam breads, used in the downstream process to manufacture car seats. Observing the downstream process steps lead to interesting discoveries:

- After transport, the packed foam rolls are unpacked: the packaging could prove to be unnecessary (temporary)? It serves to protect the dry foam bread from the weather during transport.

- The next step in making the seats is to moisten the foam bread! Indeed, the handling of the dry foam does not allow them to be correctly positioned ... Drying upstream could also prove to be unnecessary (temporary)? It serves to facilitate the conformity of the foam bread on delivery, which is invoiced according to their density and therefore weighed with a maximum moisture content. This observation obviously makes it possible to imagine carrying out the density test on a dried sample at the time of the test, which makes it possible to considerably limit the cost of foam cakes, which is strongly impacted by the energy required for drying, and at the same time d Eliminate the need for packaging! Drying could be limited to simple pressing, which is less expensive and avoids the humidification step of the downstream process.

System modeling thus facilitates innovation in the design of industrial processes by:

- demonstrating the usefulness of the product: transforming inputs into outputs, the

characteristics of which are useful for the downstream process and their stakeholders
- the demonstration of the usefulness (or not) of its stages and the resources consumed: participation in the rationale of the process, relationships indispensable to all stakeholders ...
- the search for "out of the box" alternatives:
    o Design adapted to the specific needs of user segments,
    o Elimination of unnecessary downstream steps,
    o Adaptation of inputs upstream,
    o Specific processing of specific inputs,
    o Necessary and sufficient solutions to meet a utility,
    o Functional benchmarks: how do we obtain the same type of performance in other industrial sectors,
    o Balancing performance between steps
    o ...

3.6 Application to product design

Let us take the example of a pen, which we are trying to improve for its manufacturer: either reduce costs or innovate to increase the potential market.

Needs: What is it for?

The utility of a pen expressed spontaneously by a user would probably be "to write".

The relations between elements:

This is not false, but the modeling system allows us to specify, by representing its relations and flows with the elements of its environment:

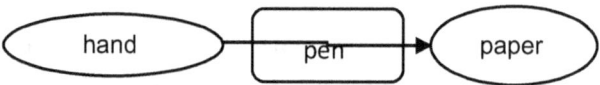

The pen allows you to write by hand on a paper. The interest of this precision? One might want to write with something else than the hand: the eye, the thought ... And write about something other than a paper. The optimal solution is obviously different according to these cases, the system modeling allows to be more precise. This will make it easier to size the pen's purpose, by dimensioning the exterior elements and the handled action: shape of the hand, type of paper, length and width of the trace ...

The expected performance of the pen - its finality - corresponds to the dimensioning of this relationship: the ergonomics of handling, the characteristics of the paper, the dimensions of the writing (length, line width, ...)

It is also possible to model the use of the pen in terms of inputs and outputs:

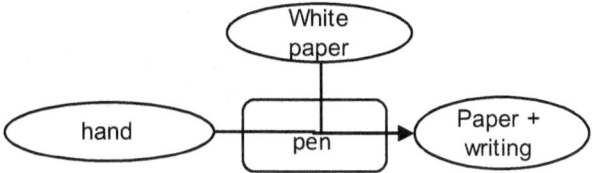

The expression of utility will be similar: allow the hand to add a trace on the paper.

"When?" ": Life cycle stages

By analyzing the relationships handled by the pen at each phase of its life cycle, the expected performances are complemented: for example (not exhaustive)

- before use: highlight the gift made by the buyer to the user

- between 2 uses: store in a pocket of the user

- at the end of life: respecting the environment

If you want to improve the value of this pen, you will want to either reduce its cost, improve its performance, or improve its performance.

"Who is it for?": Utilities for stakeholders

To improve performance, the relationship between the system and the stakeholders is sought. The system approach emphasizes the most direct involvement of stakeholders: users, suppliers, etc. Exploring needs and solutions can help them to imagine improvements.

Here, only one of the stakeholders is in contact with the pen: the hand of the sender

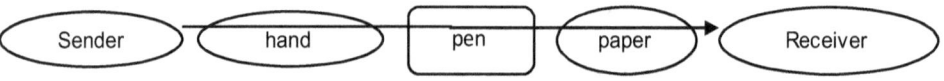

The need for the upstream stakeholder is to send a message to a receiver through the paper:

- the message could be transmitted otherwise, for example by oral communication, or via another solution, for example a computer

- depending on the specifics of the sender and receiver, the ideal transmission characteristics of the message may be different: type of writing, reading conditions ...

Resources: What is it for ?

To limit the resources consumed, we use the system modeling of the components of the pen to highlight their roles:

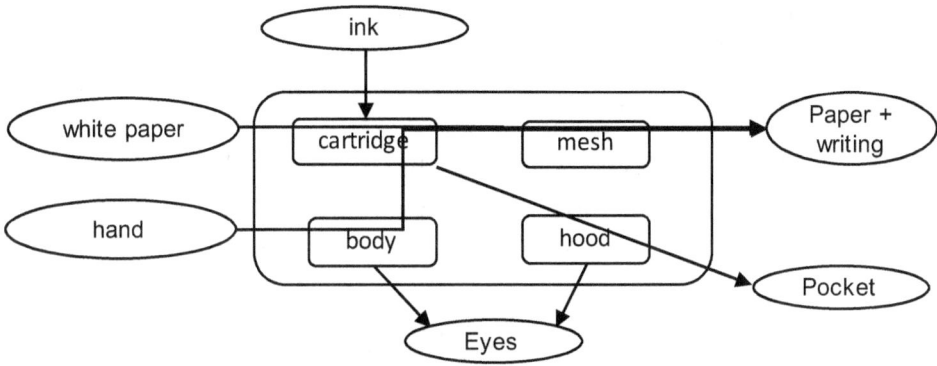

- what allows to leave a trace is the ink

- which allows the hand to hold the ink is the body

But it also highlights that other pen components have different utilities at other times in the pen life cycle:

- What is the use of the cartridge? To contain the ink, to leave a trace longer than the ink reserve

- What is the hood used for? To protect the pocket during transport between 2 uses, and / or to avoid the solvent of the ink from evaporating

- the body and cap are also used to give an image when the pen is worn

What is enough?

How to improve pen performance? By adapting the capacity of the cartridge to the actual consumption, improving the ergonomics of the body, adapting the trace to readability ...

How to reduce the cost of the pen from this system modeling? The only essential component for the purpose of the pen is the ink, which costs little. And many means are devoted to other utilities, for example for aesthetics. The systematic search for the simplest means to satisfy every utility opens up paths of innovation:

> The designer will be able to choose other aesthetic means for certain audiences: an "ecological" pen with a body and a hood made of recycled cardboard? The cost will be much lower, for a much-improved utility for this target!

> Another radical innovation becomes imaginable: to leave a trace, just a pigment! The other pen components - cartridge, body, cap - are only necessary because the pigment has been chosen to be included in a solvent: a liquid ink. It is also noted that the main cause of replacement of markers for whiteboards or paperboards is the evaporation of the solvent, whereas a large part of the

pigment is still present in the tank but rendered unavailable .... A solid ink would not require a body or cartridge, or even a cap, and would not be sensitive to dryness? There are submarine archaeologists who use pastels to write ... Astronauts, who have to write in weightlessness, have also used pencils, before industrialists have developed pens for them with pressure cartridges. Has forgotten the original simple solution ...

System modeling thus facilitates innovation in product design by:

- highlighting the usefulness of the product: relations with its environment serving its stakeholders

- highlighting the usefulness (or otherwise) of the resources that make up it: participation in the raison d'être of the product, relationships indispensable to all stakeholders ...

The search for alternatives "out of the box": design adapted to user segments, necessary and sufficient solutions to meet a utility ...

3.7 Application to vocational training

Is the application of the Value(s) approach possible and relevant for management and human resources issues? We will show its effectiveness for a project to optimize the training budget of a company yet endowed with a professional HR Department and an internal training team.

A subsidiary of 1000 people of a French group wanted to optimize its budget "training": 600K € / year. Not that this budget is too large: the HRD is proud enough to spend 7.5% of the wage bill ... but it suffers budget overruns every year and feels that it does not control the profitability of this investment.

A small working group, bringing together the Training Manager, a sales force manager (a large consumer of training) and a project manager, choose to apply Value(s) thinking to this issue:

- defining a needs reference framework: "training, what is it used for? ", In order to identify the services to render and those badly rendered;

- identify unnecessary or too high costs: "training, what does it cost? "In order to identify the principles that make the services expected at the least cost.

Needs: What is it for?

The answers to this question, however simple it may be, have led the participants to interesting findings and allowed the rediscovery of the role of training.

The relations between elements:

The system modeling allows us to formalize what formation is, by representing its relations and flows with the elements of its environment:

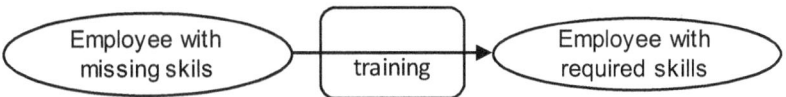

Training - adapting the skills of the staff - is one of the principles available - among others - for a company to have new skills: were the gaps measured by reference? Alternative principles have been systematically considered, despite their relevance in some cases: hiring, subcontracting, internship, internal mobility ...

The adaptation of available skills is one of the principles - among others - which the company has to adapt to changes in its environment. In most cases, action on skills must be accompanied (and sometimes even replaced) by adapting tools, methods and financial means. Are they available and adapted?

Other motivational levers exist to increase the performance of staff: status, career, remuneration, working conditions ... Have they been studied and dismissed? How many training projects fail to take into account these complementary factors: no career plan, no overloading of work and loss of productivity linked to learning ...

"Who is it for? ": Utilities for stakeholders

The training is therefore used by existing staff to acquire new skills, to adapt the company to a changing environment. But it obviously serves other stakeholders! The modeling of the elements of the system makes it possible to highlight them:

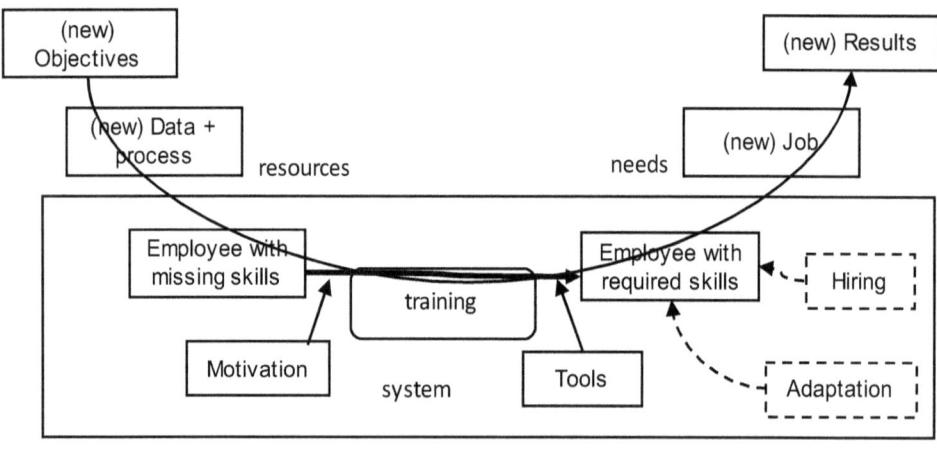

The training makes it possible to adapt the skills of the employee to implement the processes necessary to the achievement of the objectives of the company, through the manager in charge.

And it is only one of the means available to do this: be careful not to neglect others!

Other reasons may be the result of training: responding to a request from staff, creating a common mindset ... These goals are acceptable, IF they serve the company ... otherwise the company should not support?

"When?" ": Life cycle stages

According to researchers at the Palo Alto Institute for Research on Learning, training is a process that takes each participant through successive states: the actor begins most often "unconscious of his incompetence", an awareness must make him " Conscious of his incompetence ", to acquire readily the knowledge necessary to become" aware of his competence ". But a competence is really only acquired by being "unaware of its competence": this stage of training is very often neglected, whereas it is the only guarantee of the performance objective. The same happens for the first stage of motivation of the participants.

Not everyone learns in the same way: David Kolb has distinguished several learning styles: the divergent enjoys learning by experience; The assimilator appreciates the theoretical courses; The convergent appreciates projects and self-managed activities; The accommodator appreciates the exercises in small groups.

A complete process will therefore include the following steps:

1. Objectives "For what? The trainer introduces the subject. It specifies the pedagogical objectives of the session and integrates the wishes of the participants: what an ideal outcome
2. Anchoring: The trainer makes the participants interact, based on an exercise linked to their experience. The objective is to open the session in a participatory way and to make aware of each of its axes of progress.
3. Inputs: The trainer presents the principles, tools, methods ... drawn from the best practices of the profession.
4. Demonstration: The trainer presents a concrete case: success story ... It is to illustrate, to repeat the message in a concrete form.
5. Practice: Participants practice the tools and methods by performing an exercise in another area, followed by a topic (s) specific to the participants.
6. Appropriation: Each participant defines a field of application on which he will experiment. The

trainer and/or manager evaluates the actual application with each participant.

+ Repeat in case of deviation!

Resources: What is it for?

In deciding to launch only cost-effective training projects, it remains to choose the most economical means to achieve their objectives. The Value(s) thinking will be as follows:

- Identify significant expenses: "How much does it cost? "
- Define the reasons why they exist: "What are these expenses for? "
- Questioning solutions: "Are there other ways that are as effective and less costly? "

Expenditure related to a training project does not only concern the running of an internship, but all the stages of the project: Conception of the training / Realization of the contents, supports, tools / Provision and animation / Evaluation / Learning.

The "free" design and animation of training by employees sometimes costs more than external facilitators: salaries + charges + shortfall due to unavailability of the actors to their posts on one side. Animation internally will be preferred for other reasons: confidentiality, specific culture, training of internal experts ...

The main cost of a training being the salary of the participants, the means that save it will be favored as much as possible: self-training, training outside working time ...

What is enough?

From these new points of view, it became possible to:

> To identify all future training needs at the earliest: by identifying the adaptation projects of the company's processes. All projects do not require training, but how many "urgent" training projects arise lately in HRD, linked to projects that have been known for a long time elsewhere in the company: new products, new tools, recruitment ...

> To establish the profitability of a training: what is the stake (threat avoided, or opportunity seized) of the adaptation of the company to the evolution perceived in its environment? Additional profit, market share, increased human capital, improved working conditions ... Of course, training alone rarely achieves this result, making it difficult to calculate? Yet the effectiveness of training can be measured in relation to the issue: how much would be lost without training? The profitability of a training becomes therefore measurable, not only in relation to the pedagogical objectives but in relation to the primary goal: the adaptation of a process generating value. This profitability is often difficult to measure precisely? The important thing is to establish - with common sense and

pragmatism - the level of profitability, and its uncertainty: the cost is easy to know, the gain more uncertain.

> Therefore, to launch only profitable trainings. And do not start projects of uncertain profitability: if the gain is not well below the costs, or if the encryption has not been done ...

> No longer limit the training to the organization of internships for an internal catalog. Each project must (and can) be integrated into the overall process adaptation project and be managed by the person in charge of the overall project. The person in charge of the threatened process is the only one able to measure the stake and the profitability of the action. The training then ceases to be merely an employee right or an expense that is difficult to justify, to become a strategic lever, mastered by a manager.

> To launch training projects only if they are the best way to achieve the overall adaptation objective, checking that the other means have been discarded: hiring, internal mobility, temporary work ...

> To ensure that the conditions for success of each training are met: motivation, tools and time available to participants, real implementation, integration into strategic projects of the company, HRD ...

> To leave the annual "budget" logic, often prevailing: the company should launch all the training projects identified, if each proves profitable.

The urgency of a project - which would have led to a "budget overrun" - is no longer a relevant criterion: if it is obviously profitable, it must be invested; If it is not possible to ensure its profitability - even for lack of time to calculate the gain - it should not be risked ... Only limit, common to any investment project: the company does not necessarily have the means to To carry out all its projects, even if they are profitable:

- financial means, to buy necessary products, supports and services,

- logistical means: rooms, computers ...

- human resources: facilitators and participants.

The most limiting factor is often the availability of participants: if the objective of training is to make staff more able to generate more profits, it is not a question of preventing them from working through excessive training.

The choice to launch a training project for unavoidable reasons is always possible: organize an "exit", yield to the whim of a leader, etc. But then it became possible to arbitrate the cost ...

> To study all the principles of transmission: the training in the room is not necessarily the best principle. Self-training has already been mentioned, but other ways of transmitting knowledge and skills exist: sponsorship or coaching, paper or computerized guides or procedures, direct hands-on experience ...

> Focus on evaluation: Vocational training worthy of the name always ends with an evaluation. But watch out for what is measured: compliance with the program? The acquisition of knowledge? Achievement of educational objectives? The acquisition of a new skill? Improving the performance of a business process?

The evaluation methods are varied, in terms of cost and relevance depending on the objective: satisfaction scale, MCQ, case study, jury, assessment center, actual situation, etc.

The application of these principles is not obvious, even for a seasoned training professional. How to ensure this skill?

Results

The practical implementation of this approach was achieved through a few adaptations in the bank: the creation of an "opportunity card" for each training project, a process for identifying "latent" projects, A "training committee" and a new role for the Training Manager:

> The "training opportunity sheet" defines for each project:

- a decision-maker (operational beneficiary), the stakes (risks or opportunities and deadlines), conditions for success (other tools, management ...)

- the choice of the training among all the possible principles, its complete costs (salaries, profits ...), and its profitability (costs <<< stakes)

Its implementation for ongoing projects made it possible to identify: projects without beneficiaries (sic!), For which resources were lacking (training on a computer tool launched well before its acquisition ...), for which other means would be More efficient (hiring salespersons of a partner on a new product), or the means were disproportionate (developing in-house an electronic support of self-training to a public office tool)

> A monitoring of "latent" projects is implemented: the Training Manager interviews project managers every three months about the future needs of their projects. This process made it possible to identify about as many training projects as the Opportunity sheet had allowed to discard. The result is therefore less to reduce the estimated budget (always very easy to reduce: it is enough to limit it!) Than to avoid future overruns, or - more seriously - to penalize future projects, while retaining only Projects.

> The "training committee" meets twice a year, no longer to study the profitability of the projects, already validated at this stage, but to validate the training of the opportunity cards and to arbitrate between the projects if the resources available - Especially human - are not enough.

> The role of the Training Manager has evolved considerably: from operational subcontracting, he has become a coach for project promoters, supported by a "Guide to the design of a training action" containing the elements necessary for the expression of Need, stakes, cost, alternatives, criteria ...

3.8 Application to the educational project of a school

The same approach can be applied to any situation of negotiation, even conflict, between two persons or groups, in any field, professional or not.

A few years ago, the head of a kindergarten school was confronted with a project which she feared would generate strong confrontations: the drafting of an "educational project". Apparently innocuous, this project faces a special situation: this 'private' Catholic[12] school is home to 3 small classes in a quiet area of a small town in the west of France. Two populations entrust their cherubs to them: on the one hand the neighborhood mothers, who appreciate the proximity of this human-sized structure, and willingly discuss after class in the courtyard with sandbox and age-old maples. On the other hand, the Catholic mothers of the surrounding parish, who meet the school director and team at Sunday Mass. In addition, the Catholic local Church, managing the school under contract with the French Ministry of Education, specifically asked the school director to link the future educational project to Christian values and Scriptures.

In this context, the director fears that the debates around children education could turn badly: some of the mothers on both sides (secular / religious) could take this

---

[12] Of course, this description is not a judgement of any kind and is not representative of the author's opinion

opportunity to push school education to their own side... She therefore asks one of the parents, professional consultant, to help her as a coach, and avoid a new "religious war" ;-)

Needs: What is it for?

The first meeting to which the parents were invited confirms the risk that mothers[13] would divid into two distinct blocks ... The facilitator, who is also a pupil's parent and who has friends in both clans, is introduced by the school director. He proposes to coach a first meeting by dedicating it to only 2 questions: "What is an educational project for?" and "How to decide whether or not to select a proposal for the future educational project?". If this first meeting satisfies the participants, he would ask the participants to wait for the next meetings to make content proposals for the project. Despite a general surprise, the participants began by asking the school director about what is an *educational* project.

This should not be confused with the *pedagogical* project, which concerns student learning and must be developed by the teaching staff on the basis of the official programs and presented to the parents. The educational project concerns the principles of education that will be implemented within the school, in the relations between pupils and members of the management. The question "What is it

---

[13] No father was present ... except the facilitator

for?" then comes as the subject of a debate between the participants: the initial answer is "to educate our children", which does not relax the school director ...

The facilitator then coaches the discussions between parents and summarizes the following elements: the educational project is: a document formalizing principles to be applied by school staff to the children during their stay in school.

"Who is it for? ": Utilities for stakeholders

This question allowed a change of perspective: the document will not be used by children (who do not know how to read!) but by the educators, teachers and staff of the school. And the source of the principles of education is ... the parents themselves.

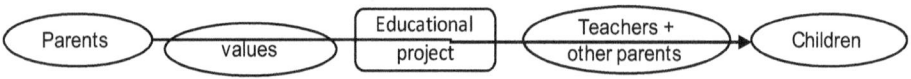

The purpose of the document is modified: it becomes the list of principles of education that all parents ask teachers to apply to their children during school time! And even to apply by parents to their own children when they are in school!

The participants, with this improved understanding of the issue, were already putting in their heads the list of principles that they will want to see applied to their youngsters... And the school director was even less relaxed at the idea of maybe being obliged to apply principles that would not be her own!?

Resources: What is it for?

A consensus being reached on this first point, the second question was addressed: "How to decide whether to select a proposal for the future educational project? ".

The facilitator chose this question to apply Value(s) thinking: the resources that must be saved here are not money, perhaps time (of discussion) but especially the negative emotions which would probably arise from meetings where everyone would try to impose to others his own educational values! What the director would like to avoid are difficult debates about the comparative virtues of educational principles. The best way to avoid unproductive debates is to put in place a collective decision rule before the proposals are made! Once this rule is accepted and put in place, any proposal may or may not be integrated into the educational project, without an outrageous debate.

The question is thus asked to all the participants: "how to select a proposal for the future educational project? ". After a short silence of reflection, one of the mothers exclaims: "Unanimously, of course! ". Everyone was first a little stunned, but an intense discussion followed: each one realized that the document will be collective, and that the same principles of education would of course apply to everyone's child! And so that each principle mentioned in the educational project must be endorsed by each parent: no parent (the dad facilitator either) will accept to leave his child in a school that would not apply the principles it shares! So the only acceptable rule to retain a principle proposed by one of the parents in the school project will be that all the others will agree! It is impossible to decide even by majority: this would mean that some parents will have imposed on others principles that they do not share? The Ministry directive also mentions the obligation for each parent to sign the future educational project when his child is enrolled in the school, whether or not he has participated in the development of the educational project. Those who do not agree will not enroll their children or will have to convince the other parents to change the educational project.

This first 2-hour meeting ended in a good mood: the questions, though they may have appeared strange at the beginning, have allowed everyone to better understand the issue, and even the director understands that the rule of deciding unanimously - if not at first imaginable - will facilitate future exchanges.

What is enough?

The next meeting aimed at collecting the parents' proposals on the principles of education to be included in the project. As a rule of decision has been already accepted, there should be no difficulty to let parents express even divergent proposals? These can be ruled out if not unanimous, and original ideas can be presented safely and accepted.

And there, surprise: none of the proposals made by parents of all styles was rejected! All the proposals made, written on the board as stated, received the unanimity of the other parents... What happened? Was the director wrong to fear tensions? Probably in some way: the proposals were all based on general principles, secular, without any connotation either religious or social. Just common principles to have well-behaved children, respectful of each other and their teachers. But later exchanges with some more 'extreme' parents showed that they understood after the first meeting that some of the proposals they had thought of initially had no chance of unanimity. And especially that these were not in line with the 'raison d'être' of the educational project in this school! Understanding the common purpose and taking into account the values of the other stakeholders has made it possible for all to avoid difficult discussions! The director confirmed her relief.

But this was not over... At the final meeting, where the formatting of the document was to be discussed - a leaflet in the shape of a small house opened to the world, with sandbox and secular maples, of course - one of the moms made a serious remark: "We have forgotten something very important! We have listed a dozen educational principles, which everyone shares, but... the Church has asked us to make explicit mention of the Scriptures! ". A huge, embarrassed silence ... at the end of which the same mother continued spontaneously (she admitted to us after not having prepared anything): "But all these principles are already there in the Scriptures ... we just have to adapt the formulation : " *Come to me little children* "," *What you will do to the least of these is to Me you will do* ", etc. ". After the meeting, the same mother finished: "No worries, I'm going to bring two or three friends together, and next time we'll present you with illustrations of our principles in New Testament verses! ". Relief of all ... and the new educational project of the school was adopted by all.

This non-professional example shows the power of the Value(s) approach in expressing stakeholder expectations, while respecting the values of each one.

Many examples exist in the professional context: buyer/seller negotiations, conflict management, ...

3.9 Application to time management

This chapter aims at improving the daily life of a person, his well-being in his everyday activities, a subject usually devoted to personal development and the balance between professional, social and private lives.

We propose to apply the questions of the Value(s) approach:

- **Needs: what is it for?**

- **Resources: What is it for?**

- **What is enough?**

The answers to this question, however simple it may be, have led hundreds of philosophers into debates far from closed ... Let us bring our stone in all humility.

Needs: What is it for?

The relations between elements:

The daily life of a person is understood here as all his activities (physical, intellectual, social ...). The question "what is it for? "Answers classical answers: answering physiological, psychological, intellectual, spiritual needs ... described by Maslow and many psychologists and philosophers.

The goal of each person will be to increase the satisfaction of these needs by minimizing the resources consumed: material, time, skills, energy ...

The system modeling makes it possible to formalize this process where the inputs are transformed into outputs.

"Who is it for? ": Utilities for stakeholders

The needs are those of the person in question, the final stakeholder. Resources are provided by other stakeholders: the family, the professional and the social. The aim of the activities is therefore to satisfy a person's needs from the resources of others: selfish vision of life? Even if this is the case, any selfish person must in any case succeed in obtaining the said resources from the persons concerned! And if they have the same "selfish" purpose of meeting their own needs, each will want to do it from the resources of others at the least cost to him. Difficult to escape this interdependence!? That was already found in the modeling of the company, which each stakeholder wishes to withdraw more than it gives.

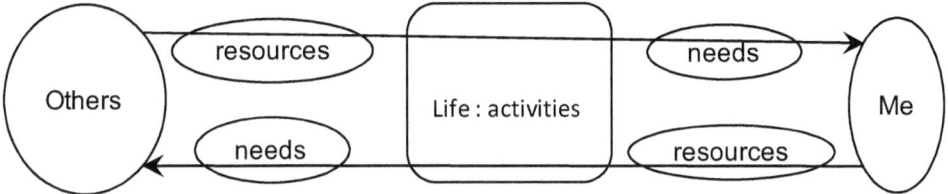

An altruistic vision of life advocates that I be interested and contribute to meet the needs of others. But it must not be at my expense! Many altruists testify that giving without waiting is very rewarding, and ensures many gifts in return, both psychological and material.

Whether one is selfish or altruistic, is it not common sense to find that the process must be iterative to last! The real difference between the two loops is that one is virtuous and bets on the long-term return, and the other secures short-term needs at the risk of drying up the source of future satisfaction.

"When?" ": Life cycle stages

The process logically leads us to study the different moments of the day (day, night ...), at different times of the year, at different times of life: it is easy to recognize that the needs are different. In practical terms, a person wants to improve his or her daily lives? It remains to be taken into account the probable evolutions of its needs in order to prepare future activities.

Resources: What is it for?

To increase the value of a person's daily activities is to improve the satisfaction of one's needs by limiting the resources consumed: time, energy, money ... If all these resources are to be saved, the one chronically lacking is certainly time? Let us focus on this point.

We can therefore analyze a day as a series of activities: we will study how each activity consumes time and apply the question "what is it for? ": How do they help meet the needs of the person? This leads to some surprising findings:

- The daily activity that consumes the most time is ... sleep! With + -8h or 1/3 of the daily time. What is the use of this "activity"? The input is a body and mind tired, transformed into body and mind rested. To do what? Go back for another day of activities ... So useless? A good way to know the usefulness of a thing is ... to deprive yourself and see what happens. Sleep is very useful ;-) But maybe we can spend less time or make it more restful?

- The work is supposed to take an important part of the time: 7h30 in France, ie +/- 1/3 of the day. But only working days, 220 days a year, or only 2/3 of the year. And only during the working period, ie theoretical 40 years, over a lifetime of more than 70 years, or ½ to 2/3 of life. This is only for those who "work" during their lives: that of mothers of families, sick, disabled ... "Work" thus takes less than 10% of the time of our lives! What is the use of this working time? Sometimes it is necessary to satisfy physiological needs directly: farmers generate food ... More often to generate financial resources that will allow the acquisition of goods and services that will answer physiological, psychological needs ... 10% of the time provides enough to live the remaining 90%: how productive!

- Daily activities also include a lot of social interaction time, with no direct professional goal. Even working time can be considered as polluted by unproductive "social" times, that is, not involved in income generation. Are these times unnecessary and should they be eliminated, especially working time? These social times serve to respond directly to our psychological needs of social animal ... Not so useless as that, so, at least for the person concerned! It is common sense. But we understand that people who give their financial resources to exchange them for productive work consider these social times useless! Unless one shows, as for sleeping time, that eliminating them leads to a significant fall in productivity. Psychosociological studies have shown that a working group consumes close to 1/3 of its time in managing social links that are not directly productive but irreducible, regardless of the mode of leadership!

- The structuring of time has an impact on its productivity: zapping has a detrimental effect on productivity, especially for men who are less multitasking than women. Similarly, there are waiting times before the start of an activity, due to the absence of the necessary conditions, tools and information. The significant difference of time spent between 2 tasks carried out in parallel or each one continuously then serves to "yield to the emergency injunctions of the stakeholders"? An analogy: test the difference one night of 7h and 7 naps of 1h!

What is enough?

How to improve the value of our limited time? The above points open up tracks:

> Seek to fulfill the needs of those most profitable to you: either those that will give you the most in return, or the most important ones to you altruistic. Everyone will draw up his list in the order that suits him: spouse, children, parents, friends, collaborators, but also neighbors, associations, minorities, coreligionists, society ... and God? To know their needs: to ask them is of course the most effective. And to observe their reactions to previous attempts: many people have difficulty expressing their real needs ... To choose the best channel of distribution, know the "love language" of your loved ones: not everyone perceives the same value in A gift, a positive word, a shared moment, a service rendered, a gesture of affection ...

> First plan important (not the most urgent!) Activities, ie responding to important needs as directly as possible, and generating the best synergies with other activities. Do not neglect sleep or physical exercise creates positive feedback loops: these activities make others more effective!

And plan first the tasks that most effectively meet the needs of people important to you, by creating other synergies: playing sports or praying with your spouse, helping your children with their homework ...

> Improving the value created during our working hours? For example, by choosing a work that is passionate, or that directly contributes to the physiological needs (shelter, food, exercise ...), psychological (recognition, positive relations, love ...), intellectual, even spiritual! Let us note, moreover, that generation Y (pronounced "why" ie "why" in English) enters the professional life with an acute awareness of the meaning of work!

> Avoid unproductive times: especially those due to bad sequencing. So, plan first the long tasks requiring concentration, avoiding to let them cut out: many techniques are proposed to avoid the tyranny of the real time, such as that of the "rendezvous with oneself". Multitasking can be efficient, however, if a wait time is spent in one activity on one productive task in another.

3.10 Application to ... the meaning of life

This last chapter has the ambition (disproportionate and illegitimate?) to contribute in an original way to the most fundamental philosophical debate, pushing Value(s) thinking to its limit. This chapter is constructed not from the experience of real projects, but from an attempt (awkward and incomplete) of applying Value(s) thinking to ... life itself? Will we find philosophical positions, which would validate the vision of the company that has emerged?

Let us first, as in the preceding chapters, set out the object we are seeking to improve: the life of a person, his whole journey from birth to death. The question: "*What is the purpose of life on earth of a person?*" could lead us to philosophical debates but let us apply Value(s) thinking.

Needs: What is it for?

The relations between elements:

The life of a person is understood here more broadly than everyday life seen in the previous chapter. Let us consider 'life' as the 'vital process' from birth to death. Value(s) thinking allowed us to considered processes before: their goal is to transform their inputs into useful outputs.

What is there upstream of the vital process? Does it start at birth or design? In any case, parents are upstream, sharing their love and their genetic material through sperm and egg to initiate the elaboration of a new living being.

This life is then deployed through material resources, first provided through the mother's placenta, then after birth through breast milk and then other foods to meet physiological needs. Other resources - intellectual, relational, spiritual ... - will be necessary to the daily life, which will end one day by a physiological failure and death.

What outputs downstream of the life process? Physiological waste, an inanimate body, social interactions, children ...

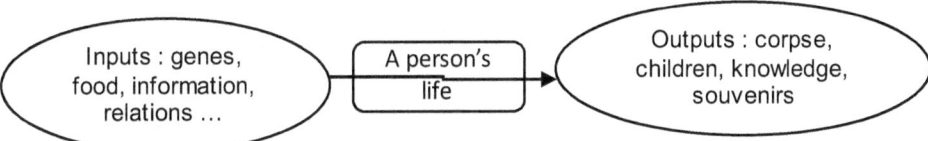

"Who is it for? ": Utilities for stakeholders

Boulding, taken up by von Bertalanffy and Le Moigne, present the human being as a "self-finalized system", which would make life an end in itself, a person who should then aim only for his own needs? The system approach considers that things are useful in their relations with their environment. A person's life would not be useful to itself, but to its stakeholders: parents, family, children, friendly and professional relations, society ... Boulding proposed levels of systems beyond the human: social And transcendental.

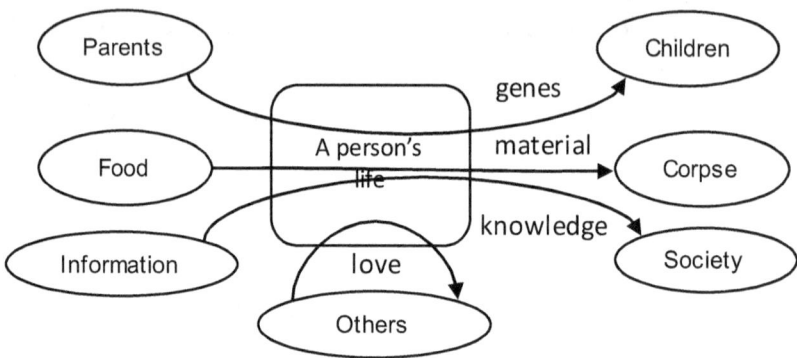

A vision of "selfish" life is supported by libertarians: Harry Browne argued in 1973 that "selfishness is the only relevant motor for man, whose goal is personal freedom. He must free himself from all the mental limitations imposed on him by society, by the government, and by his own erroneous vision of the world. " This book is with "Atlas Shrugged" by Ayn Rand, the originator of the libertarian movement still very powerful in the United States: several presidents refer to it and until Steve Jobs would have discovered his vocation by reading Ayn Rand, whose book Would be the most read in the US after the Bible ... A very positive point in my eyes: the realization that "A consciously selfish individual is sensitive to the needs and desires of others. He does not, however, consider these as demands, but as opportunities for potential transactions to make both parties happier! Let us accept this interdependence, and the way is free ;-) towards the quality of relationships and the positive emotions of all parties, which reinforce each other! Some call it altruism ... according to who begins: me or the others? As blogger Damien Casoni summarizes in our discussions: "The altruist will realize the importance of a fluid and powerful ego to truly help others. And the selfish will understand the need to open up and offer himself to grow more. "

Here we see the same change of perspective as for the company, which does not serve for itself (who?) But for its external stakeholders. This is also true for any human group: association, clan, country ...

One could express this process as the transformation of flows exchanged with the stakeholders. The goals of life then become:

- transmitting the genetic material of the parents to the children (this is Dawkins 'and GC Williams' theory of self-annoyance)
- to transform mineral matter (water, air ...) and organic (food) into organic matter (inanimate body)
- to generate new works and knowledge from materials and information

- generate psychological (emotional) and spiritual (love) relationships with other people

As with the company, the priority of one of these goals over others is a matter of choice, one cannot be achieved in isolation: genes and love will not be transmitted without ensuring the body's nourishment ...

Resources: What is it for?

What resources do you want to save to improve a person's life? The efforts of body and mind to feed, to seduce a genetic partner, to leave an intellectual, emotional and spiritual trace ... But what is the objective: happiness? Can it be expressed in other words? Let us take a step back.

"Life" is not limited to every person, not even humans. Science tells us that it did not appear right away in the history of the world, but after a long evolution, starting from inanimate matter. Even without going so far as to find it meaningful-a sense-, evolution therefore has a direction - a meaning!

It seems important here to emphasize the importance of collaboration, exchange, sharing ... at each stage of evolution: properties emerge at each level of pooling!

- molecules have properties which do not have the atoms that compose them: for example, water, such a simple molecule, has solvent properties

fundamental to life but inaccessible to the hydrogen or the oxygen which compose it. And the water molecule, like the others, is formed by the sharing of electrons between its atoms!
- assembled molecules form mineral materials
- molecules assembled in specific ways (amino acids, DNA ...) give rise to living beings, which know how to develop, reproduce ... it is the organization of molecules that differentiates living matter!
- living cells assembled form multicellular beings, and succeed better by specializing and sharing among themselves the result of their specific activities
- specialization leads to tissues that form organs with specific roles in more evolved living beings: the initial universal potential of each stem cell is abandoned to become specialized cells that together and increase their chances of survival Know the parable of the organs that believe each one to be superior to the others, until the anus strikes?)
- living beings live in society where they choose specialized roles and exchange with others for greater chances of survival
- sexual reproduction, where individuals differ in order to procreate by exchanging their differences,

ensures more success to the lineage than asexual reproduction: parthenogenesis
- symbiosis is formed between species, where each brings to the other
- ecosystems are formed, where the waste of one is the resources of the others and the balance is carefully maintained by feedback loops
- humans form societies (other names of companies) where they pool their resources (money, time, skill, products ...) to serve clients' needs and get more (money, status, recognition ...).) Than what they put there ...
- couples form and associate in the long term, losing each their autonomy, to better protect their heritage and their offspring
- social groups (families, clans, tribes, nations, etc.) are formed, where respect for each one of the rules chosen together (rights and reciprocal duties) leads to loss of freedom by gaining security and synergy
- etc.

Obviously, there are examples of backtracking:

- living beings live independently, freely taking away the resources made available by other beings who are often more evolved, even if it means exhausting their host: this is called parasitism!
- even the cells of a living being can return to their original freedom, become all-powerful again, draw

freely from the available resources without worrying about a so-called common good ...: this is called cancer!

Many scientists, different confessions or atheists, have worked to bring out a unified and coherent vision of the world by bringing together, after centuries of separation, our rational knowledge and the intuitions of the great spiritual traditions.

For example, understanding the world has been profoundly affected by the validation of quantum mechanics: observation, so consciousness affects observation, to the point that certain physicists do not hesitate to conclude that reality does not exist without The observation therefore the consciousness! And that the interactions between elementary particles make the world one and not composed of distinct elements. These conclusions, which have shaken even Einstein of other physicists nevertheless at the origin of these theories, join the visions of the world of many religions and philosophies.

What is next?

Does evolution end with us? Is not it presumptuous to believe it, as men of every age must have considered themselves the ultimate outcome! But then where is she going? Obviously more collaboration, exchange, sharing ... in wider social groups, through more effective means of communication, aiming for better relations between people and with the inanimate world that makes their subsistence!

What about transhumanism? The fusion of technology and biology seems inescapable, as well as the advent of artificial intelligence. The "connected" man seems dehumanized, but how do the protozoa, the "free" individual cells, see the "connected" cells of the animal organs? ... The deprivation of freedom brought about by the technology of electrical communication between the Neurons should seem unacceptable to free cells? But let's not push the allegory too far ...

Will it emerge from other properties of these future pools? Probably, even if it is difficult to imagine them, how difficult it is for a cell to imagine the organ of which it is a part?

But it is probable that these are spiritual dimensions: the movement of life emerges from the individualized matter, culminates today in consciousness and the global, tends towards more spirit?

After the individual consciousness, which alone allows man to find meaning in things, does life develop into a new meaning, a collective consciousness? The future will tell.

Some, believing in "something else" than the material world, see it as a support for the spirit: the body (or its draft) would receive the "soul" to form a living person, and free it to death from the body? Life is thus a process of maturation of the soul, coming from elsewhere and returning to it, confronted during life by experiments in which it can be transformed, enlarged or not. The meaning of life would then be to take advantage of the confrontation with other souls through bodies: for what? Many religions, philosophies and wisdom agree on one goal: love (agape), the ultimate form of collaboration and sharing among humans.

Is it not surprising that science and spirituality bring us back to the same thing?

Part 4 - Existing Value(s) methods

The book "Valeur(s) & Management"[14] presented some twenty methods already present in companies to improve performance at all levels. A more systematic inventory was carried out via the LinkedIn Value(s) & Management network, which brings together more than 600 members in March 2015. A hundred or so methods have been identified that share some or all of these concepts, more or less explicitly.

The aim of this work is to present the value concepts that are common to them, and which gives them their effectiveness, linked to the system approach that they decline and make operational in their field of application. The identification of these common concepts makes it possible both to make possible synergies between these methods, which are too often local, and sometimes to add to them.

It seemed relevant to work on the exploration of these methods, to highlight their link with Value(s) thinking, and to suggest ways to further strengthen them. The details of this work are included in the valuesandmanagement.com blog, to which the interested reader can refer and contribute: synergies are possible

---

[14] « Valeur(s) & Management : des méthodes pour plus de valeurs dans le management » by Olaf de Hemmer and Hugues Poissonnier, EMS Ed° 2013

between these methods, to implement Value(s) thinking at all levels.

Obviously, it is not a matter of replacing the specialists in these methods, who retain their full legitimacy! Neither propose to replace these methods with others. But to reinforce their relevance and to open the way for specialists, the introduction of this book underlines the obvious value of having a coherent set of methods to improve the performance of organizations in synergy and to avoid Quarrels of chapels or work in silos, which prevents collaborative work and the search for common sense.

More than one hundred Value(s) methods have been identified[15]:

- Activity Based Costing – ABC
- Agile methods / Scrum
- AVID - Analysis of the Value Applied to Information and Documentation
- Balanced Score Card - BSC
- Benchmarking
- Benefit Corporation - BCorp
- Blue Ocean - Blue Ocean Strategy
- Business Analysis - BA
- Business Model Generation / Canvas
- Business Process Management - BPM

---

[15] For a complete list (in French, sorry) see http://valeursetmanagement.com/quoi/

- Business Mapping
- Circular economy
- Co-creative Negotiation ™
- Commons management
- Concurrent Engineering
- Conscious capitalism
- Collaborative economy
- Corporate Social Responsibility - CSR
- Cradle to cradle
- Customer Value Added
- Customer Experience Management - CEM
- Design for Value
- Design Thinking
- Design To Cost / Time / X – DTC/T/X
- Earned Value Management - EVM
- Eco-design
- Eco-innovation
- Economic Value Added - EVA
- Economy of functionality
- Efficiency
- Employee Experience
- Entrepreneurial Value
- European Foundation for Quality Management - EFQM
- Experiential Marketing
- Five Flows
- FMECA - Failure Modes, Effects and Criticality Analysis
- Fractal organization
- Ghandian engineering
- 'Good Enough' Revolution
- GPS by CJD – Cercle des Jeuenes Dirigeants
- Green Value Management

- GROW coaching & problem solving
- Holacraty ™
- Human Value Management
- Inclusive capitalism
- Focus on priorities
- Frugal innovation - Frugal innovation
- Interactifs Discipline®
- Jugaad innovation
- Languages of love
- Leadership through Values, Responsible Leadership
- Lean management
- Lean manufacturing
- Lean StartUp
- Learning Organization
- Long Term Value accounting
- Management 3.0
- MAREVA
- Mars and Venus
- Non Violent Communication – NVC
- Open innovation
- Oström Rules, see Commons Management
- PAT Mirror
- Positive economy
- Post-materialist science
- Process control
- Public Value Management
- Purpose management
- Radical Innovation Design
- Reconstructionism
- Redesign To Cost (s) - RTC
- SCOS'D by Ecole Centrale de Paris
- Scrum

- Shared value
- Shareholder Value
- Six Sigma
- Slow management
- Social & Sustainable Investment
- SocioDynamic
- Socrates' 3 strainers
- Solution Focus
- Supplier Relationship Management - SRM
- Surcentration
- Sustainable Development - SD
- Sustainable supply chain and operations
- Systems Engineering - SE
- Target costing - Genka Kikaku
- Theory of Constraints - TOC
- "think out of the box" creativity
- Total Cost Management - TCM
- TRIZ
- Ubuntu
- V3-vision, values and will
- Value Analysis / Engineering / Management – VA / VE / VM
- Value Based Business
- Value chain
- Value creation through purchases
- Value creation by HR
- Value Mapping Tool
- Value Marketing
- Value Perceived by Customer - VUPC
- Value proposition design
- Value Stream Mapping - VSM

This inventory is not exhaustive: our readers will be able to help us to identify others, to highlight Value(s) thinking and the system approach, and to work to their application in synergy.

What next?

The ambition of this book is to highlight the common mindset underlying many of the methods developed to improve performance at all levels of the company, to link it to scientific foundations in system thinking, explaining its originality and effectiveness, and showing that the application of simple questioning makes it possible to open amazing improvements in all these fields (the examples presented are taken from real consulting projects).

We believe this reasoning can serve as a 'meta-method' for a new approach to problem solving and management:

- Make sense by define purpose and goals, with the question "**What is it for?** "
- Innovate in a radical way by finding "**What is enough?** " to achieve what it is for, which maximizes utility and minimizes costs.
- To mobilize collective intelligence by "**working WITH the stakeholders**"

To facilitate the collective implementation of this questioning, it will probably be necessary to be assisted by tools ensuring a methodical questioning and allowing a shared representation of the reasoning. Most of these tools exist in the Value(s) methods already in use in each domain, presented in "Valeur(s) & Management"[16]. Of course, tools have been used to carry out the projects presented in these pages.

A common tool was used throughout these pages: *system modeling*, which formalizes the relations and flows between the elements of the solution studied and its environment, to the stakeholders. This tool is a canvas from which any problem can be studied and any solution imagined: try it?

The next step is to build synergies between methods, by combining the tools existing in each domain, based on the experience of the actors already at work and the common principles of the system approach: a new wave of methods!

To go further, join us:

- Participate to the Value University each year in Switzerland http://www.valueuniversity.org,
- Share with us (in French and English) your insights, methods, comments via the LinkedIn group Valeur(s) & Management: more than 1300 members!
- Contribute to the Value(s) methods inventory on the V&M blog http://valeursetmanagement.com/

---

[16] « Valeur(s) & Management » Olaf de Hemmer Gudme et Hugues Poissonnier, Ed° EMS 2013 et 2017

For any direct question, notice, comment, please email the author at:

odehemmer@valeursetmanagement.com

Table des matières

Part 1 - Value(s) thinking 9
    The 5-legged sheep 9
    The 3 Value(s) principles... 14
Part 2 – Common concepts of Value(s) methods 25
    Value/system methods:.. 26
    Value vs Values 33
Part 3 - Applications of Value(s) thinking...................... 39
    3.1 Application to a business 40
    3.2 Application to a production unit 64
    3.3 Application to a business function: Purchasing 74
    3.4 Application to an information process 86
    3.5 Application to an industrial process 93
    3.6 Application to product design 100
    3.7 Application to vocational training 106
    3.8 Application to the educational project of a school 118
    3.9 Application to time management 125
    3.10 Application to … the meaning of life 132
Part 4 - Existing Value(s) methods 142
What next? 148

www.ingramcontent.com/pod-product-compliance
Lightning Source LLC
Chambersburg PA
CBHW052300220526
45471CB00001B/423